Battleground Europe

GALLIPOLI
GULLY RAVINE

Battleground Europe
GALLIPOLI
GULLY RAVINE

Stephen Chambers

Series Editor
Nigel Cave

LEO COOPER

First published in 2003 by
LEO COOPER
an imprint of
Pen & Sword Books Limited
47 Church Street, Barnsley, South Yorkshire S70 2AS

Copyright © Stephen Chambers
ISBN 0 85052 923 9

A CIP catalogue record of this book is available
from the British Library

Printed by CPI UK.

For up-to-date information on other titles produced under the Leo Cooper imprint,
please telephone or write to:

Pen & Sword Books Ltd, FREEPOST, 47 Church Street
Barnsley, South Yorkshire S70 2AS
Telephone 01226 734222

CONTENTS

INTRODUCTION BY SERIES EDITOR

In the May of 2000 I, along with my father, was fortunate enough to go on one of Len Sellers' excellent Royal Naval Division tours of Gallipoli, a place where I must say I had never thought I would have a chance to visit. It was a wonderful introduction to a most beautiful part of the world, unspoilt, almost biblical countryside, but now strongly tinged with the haunting events that took place there in 1915. It was during this tour that I first met Steve Chambers, with his great wealth of knowledge and enthusiasm for the men and the battlefield of Gallipoli. An author to fill the gap in the *Battleground Europe* series had been found, someone to develop the trail in the series that had been commenced by Nigel Steel.

Part of our tour took us for a long walk through Gully Ravine, an extraordinarily evocative site. Although we had general details about what took place here, and some particular points could be easily pointed out, there was so much that we were missing. The result is this book. I had the great pleasure of spending a fortnight with Steve as he worked on this book in September 2001 (and we prepared the basis for future works) and I can testify to the enormous care that he took in placing the ground against the trench maps – not as easy as it might sound. Heroic sallies were made through very inhospitable undergrowth and down steep slopes, more often than not rewarded by the discovery of some trench line or mine crater. Wonderful new perspectives of the battlefield were revealed; and distractions aplenty arose from the breathtaking scenery – a scenery seemingly exclusively for our pleasure.

The result of these tours and much hard work, as well as a most impressive private collection and an understanding wife, is this first rate addition to the series. Now it is no longer a matter of coming across a deep trench line or finding an artefact; now it is possible to have a greater understanding of the extraordinary heroism displayed by both sides in that ill-fated Expeditionary action. Gully Ravine must rank with Serre and Mametz Wood on the Somme, both still relatively tranquil and quiet spots, in its capacity to move the emotions. This book will go a long way to providing the who, the why and the experiences of men (admittedly from only one side) who fought there.

Nigel Cave
Collegio Rosmini, Stresa

Sandbag dugouts, June 1915. (© Chambers)

AUTHOR'S INTRODUCTION

The Allied objective in the Gallipoli Campaign was, by capturing Istanbul (then called Constantinople), to force Germany's ally, Turkey and its Ottoman Empire, out of the war. This would open an ice-free sea supply route from the Aegean through the Dardanelles and into the Black Sea to Russia. As well as helping their beleaguered ally Russia, it would also serve the purpose of opening another front against Germany and Austria-Hungary.

The campaign fell into four phases. The first composed the naval operations of early 1915 culminating, on 18 March, in the unsuccessful attempt by British and French battleships to force a path through the Dardanelles.

The second was the landings, beginning on 25 April, by the British and French armies on Cape Helles, and by the Australian and New Zealand Army Corps on what became known as Anzac, north of Gaba Tepe. By early June the Allied force at Helles had made a few advances, but still had not captured Achi Baba or the village of Krithia, their objectives for the first day. At Anzac the situation was even worse; owing to precipitous and strongly defended terrain, no advance was possible, leaving the troops clinging onto the cliff faces on their narrow beachhead.

A panoramic shot of Gully Ravine entrance, September 1915. (IWM Q13400A)

In the third phase the British made a further landing at Suvla, just north of Anzac, on 6 August 1915, simultaneously with offensives at Helles and Anzac. This operation came near to success, but soon became deadlocked in static trench warfare.

The fourth phase, the withdrawal, saw the Peninsula evacuated, first at Anzac and Suvla on the nights of 19/20 December 1915, and then Helles on 8/9 January 1916. After eight months of campaigning the Allies had sustained a quarter of a million casualties, whilst the Turkish losses were estimated at nearer a third of a million.

Today, many people link the Gallipoli campaign with the Australians and New Zealanders. I have often heard people say, 'Gallipoli, that's where the Australians fought': many do not realise that the British and French fought there, to say nothing of the Indians, Irish, Newfoundlanders and French Africans. Anzac day, 25 April, is a national holiday in Australia and New Zealand, and many visitors to modern-day Gallipoli tend to be from those nationalities. Gallipoli is important to them, as it was here that the spirit of a nation was helped forged. Many visitors make a brief visit to Anzac, today a national park set in one of the most magnificent and picturesque landscapes on the peninsula. Few venture to Suvla, only slightly north of Anzac, and even fewer to the Helles battlefields in the south.

The whole of the peninsula has recently been declared a national historical 'Peace Park' by the Turkish authorities, designed to preserve this area of unique heritage and natural beauty for future generations.

A dump near the mouth of Gully Ravine, 1915. (© Chambers)

Helles, with its views across the Dardanelles to Achilles' tomb on Mount Orkanie, and the seven cities of Troy, as immortalised in Homer's *Iliad*, is a battlefield that also has an immense sense of tragedy, and which still shows the scars of war from almost a century ago. It was said by Brigadier-General Sir Hugh Simpson Baikie that Helles was 'one of England's greatest tragedies, but was also one of England's greatest glories'.

This book concentrates on Gully Ravine, one of those forgotten areas of Gallipoli, on the western side of the Helles battlefield. Here trench fighting raged throughout the campaign, culminating in the Battle of Gully Ravine between 28 June and 5 July 1915. This attack was a successful piece of planning and execution, enabling the British to capture five lines of Turkish trenches, which seriously threatened the Turkish hold on the southern tip of the peninsula. General de Lisle recalled,

> *in my nine years of war I have seen many thrilling sights but not one compared to the 28th June. Its success was well nigh*

Gully Ravine entrance today. (© Chambers)

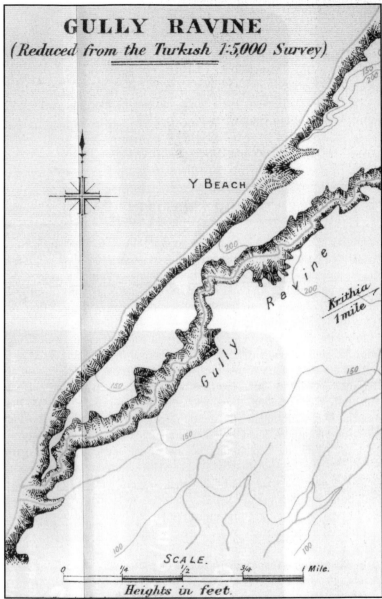

GULLY RAVINE
(Reduced from the Turkish 1:5,000 Survey)

Y BEACH

200

Ravine

Krithia
1 mile

200

Gully

150

150

150

150

100

100

SCALE.

0   1/4   1/2   3/4   1 Mile.

Heights in feet.

Map 1. General view of Gully Ravine from a War Office map, 1915.

> *complete, and the troops appeared to move with the assurance of victory.*

After this attack the region fell again into the deadlock of trench warfare, which brought its horrors as well as its monotony. Many books and guides on Gallipoli have only given Gully Ravine a brief mention, if at all, and then rarely more than a page or two. The area is seldom visited; Gully life today is usually a local picnicker sitting in the shade of the Nuri Yamut memorial or a lonely goatherd tending his flock up on Gully Spur.

This book is dedicated to all those who fought, bled and died there, from Johnny Turk to Tommy Atkins.

THEIR GLORY SHALL NOT BE BLOTTED OUT

GULLY RAVINE

During the immense heat of the summer, there is often a pleasant breeze that comes in off the sea, cooling the weary traveller. The olive and fig trees bear their fruit, whilst blossoming cotton intersperses the corn-scattered fields. The odd sound of birdsong or a tractor is all that breaks the silence; a profound silence that many visitors find so powerful as to be intimidating.

From the ridge top at Gully Ravine you can witness the sun rising from the golden plains of ancient Troy, across the Dardanelles to the east. In the west, you can see the islands of Imbros, once the home of Hamilton's GHQ, and Samothrace nestled behind in the haze. Both peacefully disappear into the shadows as the sun sets far out into the Aegean. Ever-daunting are the gentle slopes that rise gently up to Achi Baba (un-captured Allied Objective), looking so close, but teasingly so far away. With the outstanding beauty of the area, it is clear why bathing in the Aegean Sea was likened to a holiday at the beach. During the campaign, rains of shrapnel, snipers' bullets and the odd shell broke into this paradise. Today there are no snipers or shells, just the peace, grandeur and romanticism of an old battlefield.

Ellis Ashmead-Bartlett, War Correspondent for the London Press in 1915, describes Gully Ravine:

> *But for the grimmer business of war, you would naturally stop and admire the surprising beauty of the scene, which resembles the Highlands in its rugged grandeur. The heat in summer is, however, almost unbearable, because the sea breezes penetrate its depths, and the sun beats down on this war-worn road with pitiless severity. But there is plenty of good water for men and horses, parched by the sun and the sand. These springs are carefully guarded against pollution, and are known and beloved by every thirsty warrior to, or on his way from, the trenches. There are some which, flowing from the interior of the hills, enter*

the valley in a tiny, trickling stream, clear as crystal and icy cold. Crowds of perspiring, dusty, thirsty, men will wait indefinite periods in a long queue, each with his water-bottle in hand, for the privilege of obtaining a draught from one of these springs, which are valued more in Gallipoli than the choicest brand of champagne would be at home...Along the road in every spot sheltered by the overhanging cliffs from the sun you will find hundreds of weary men who have just come from the trenches, and who have flung themselves down to snatch a few hours' sleep whilst they may. They lie there unconscious and indifferent to the shells bursting overhead and the stream of bullets, which come 'sizzling' along. A man drops and is immediately carried to the dressing station, but no one takes the smallest notice or even seeks cover, for prolonged experience has had the effect of making nearly all indifferent or fatalists. In the ravine you are constantly coming upon lonely graves, each marked with a cross and a name, marking the last resting-place of some soldier who has fallen in one of the early engagements, or who has been killed on his way to the front and who has been buried just where he fell.[1]

These gully-dwellers, living their troglodyte existence, gained some cover in caves and shelters dug into the sides of the cliffs and gullies. This was one of the few areas on the Helles front that offered any serious protection from the Turkish shellfire, as shells seldom dropped into the ravine depths. However, all were recommended to keep to the eastern side of the ravine as the western side was constantly swept with bullets, aimed and spent, that flew overhead from the firing lines above. Reverend Oswin Creighton, Chaplain to 86 Brigade, describes this danger, his dugout being

Aberdeen Gully, site of 89/Field Ambulance dressing station. The path runs up into a little natural amphitheatre in the cliff, about fifteen yards in diameter. (© Chambers)

> *...about 500 yards from the firing line in a little gully called Aberdeen Gully (as the 89th come from there), which runs off the big gully. A narrow path about fifty yards long had been cut out of the*

13

bed formed by a stream, now dry. The path runs up into a little natural amphitheatre in the cliff, about fifteen yards in diameter. The sides of the gully are almost precipitous, but it had been widened enough at places to make a dressing-station, cookhouse, and officers mess, and the amphitheatre is also used as a dressing station if necessary. It is absolutely safe, but bullets have a way of dropping anywhere, and a man got one in his arm last night, and one was at the foot of my dugout this morning. My dugout is reached by a little flight of steps partly cut out of the soft rock and partly made of sandbags. It is only just long enough for me and is cut into the rock with a piece of corrugated iron as cover. It is very snug and away from people, and I sleep on pine branches.[2]

In the shelter of the gully, the noise during a bombardment would have sounded through the ravine like an express train. When Arthur Behrend, a Lieutenant in the 4/East Lancashire Regiment, arrived in the gully, he recalls:

...our own shells tore overhead too, filling the Gully with a hollow blasting roar which echoed and re-echoed from side to side for hundreds of yards. A dry and sandy stream bed ran conveniently along the bottom and formed a ready-made road; as we marched, still in single file, there was plenty to see – ambulances, dressing stations, Indians and their goats, even a general or two.[3]

The only gully-dwellers today are the fox or jackal, in their holes by day, a sunbathing lizard or the odd tortoise. The cliffs along the coast also provided a temporary home for the troops. Between Fusilier Bluff and Trolley Ravine, Lieutenant Melville Hamilton, attached 1/Border Regiment, wrote a letter home dated 1 August 1915:

Now we have moved right over to the left flank and are in support. We are in dugouts in a hillside facing the sea and if there were not so many bullets and so much dust and flies about it would be quite a nice spot...it is when being here, within a few yards of the sea and not being able to go and bathe in it, but the shore in this part is all under Turkish fire.

During the campaign the gully was like a bustling town, with its terraced dugouts, scattered little cemeteries, open canvas dressing stations, headquarters and numerous supply dumps. Deep inside the ravine, the dry, sandy, streambed road paved the way for horse-drawn ambulances, busy stretcher-bearers and marching troops. This road wound its way gently up to a steep zigzagging path that climbed up the cliff face and into the firing lines.

During the night the horror and grim reality of war did not go away for the men, even though night did offer some sort of relief, if not from the bullets, then from the heat of the sun. A thousand tiny flickering lights lined the tiers of dugouts, giving the place a more romantic look, a 'Mediterranean Blackpool' as some described it. Twilight must have seemed peaceful with the sound of the Aegean lazily lapping against the coast, whilst the sunset glowed deep red behind the island of Imbros, finally disappearing behind the snow-tipped mountains of distant Samothrace. Today the war has gone, but the modern-day traveller can still experience the same sun, stars and sea, in the footsteps of those distant soldiers in an age now past:

> *And we shall no more see the great ships gather,*
> *Nor hear their thunderings on days of state,*
> *Nor toil from trenches in an honest lather,*
> *To magic swimmings in a perfect strait,*
> *Nor sip Greek wine and see the slow sun dropping,*
> *On gorgeous evenings over Imbros Isle,*
> *While up the hill the maxim will keep popping,*
> *And the men sing and camp fires wink awhile.*
>
> SUB-LIEUTENANT AUBREY P HERBERT (HAWKE BN., RND)

ACKNOWLEDGEMENTS

Thanks are due to a number of individuals and organisations that have helped the coming about of this book. I would like to especially thank Nigel Cave for his encouragement, and his companionship on recent Gallipoli trips. Other people I am indebted too include Len Sellers and Kieran Hegarty who I accompanied on a great trip to Gallipoli in 2000, which included a memorable hike up and down Gully Ravine with some other enthusiastic gentlemen. I am also

Troops waiting in Gully Ravine. (© Chambers)

grateful to Patrick Gariepy for information on Gallipoli casualties, Alan Osborn for permission to quote from Moriarty's diary, Vera Murray for permission to quote from Joseph Murray's book, Patrick Robeson, Lieutenant-Colonel R. P. Mason, Gavin Edgerley-Harris, Ted Peacock, the Gallipoli Association and many of its members. The staff at Pen & Sword, the Public Records Office, the County Archivist, West Sussex Records Office and the Royal Sussex Regiment Trustees, the Imperial War Museum and the Commonwealth War Graves Commission, have all been of immense help, not forgetting the many regimental museums and associations, in particular the Royal Scots, Gurkha Regiment and Royal Engineers, all of whom I am greatly indebted to. In Turkey, I would like to thank Erol Baycan and his wife for a providing great hospitality and a wonderful base to work from when in Gallipoli, and their son Jon Baycan, who is currently working for the CWGC on the Peninsula. Last, but by no means least, my wife Joanne who has encouraged me when needed, and been generous with her patience. To all these people, and any I have mistakenly forgotten to mention, please accept my sincere thanks.

This book would not have been possible to write without contemporary material: war diaries, divisional, regimental and battalion histories and the excellent Gallipoli Official History by Aspinall-Oglander. I have also referenced many personal accounts in the form of letters and diaries as well as a large assortment of maps and photographs, many never having been published before. The originators of these must all be thanked, because without this material there would be no book. Any copyright holders I have not been able to trace, please accept my apologies, and feel free to contact me if you feel it necessary. I have sought to tell the story of Gully Ravine and its climatic battle on 28 June 1915 using this wealth of information, but unfortunately, due to the limited space available, please be assured that the omission of any regiment, key individual or event does in no way suggest that their part at Gully Ravine had little or no significance.

Helles Memorial to the Missing.
(© Chambers)

ADVICE TO TRAVELLERS

Stop O passer by
This earth you thus tread unawares
Is where an age lies
Bow and listen. This quiet mound
Is where the heart of a nation sighs

BY POET NECMETTIN HALIL ONAN

The best time to visit Gallipoli is between April and October. Outside this period the weather can get very wintry, cold and wet. In the spring, Gallipoli is covered by numerous wild flowers; smothered with a profusion of red poppies, white daisies and blue larkspurs. This fertile land is scattered with fields growing crops; wheat, sunflowers, melon and cotton, a very different picture to the one you may conjure up from reading books or browsing through photographs of the Gallipoli campaign. However, during the April landings this area was just as fertile as before war savaged the land. During the height of summer, between June and August, the weather is baking hot, and on most days the temperature goes well into the red. September and October are slightly cooler and thus good months to visit, the summer leaving the ground barren and sun-baked, hardened under foot, reminiscent of the 1915 period. During these months the scars of the old battlefield are sometimes visible, as crops are harvested, and the grass sun-scorched and all but gone. All that remains are the hardy scrub and the scattering of pine trees. Do not forget that the region is remote, and whilst some of the roads are good, many are in disrepair or literally dusty dirt tracks. In the wet season these can quickly turn into a quagmire, even after the lightest shower of rain. Gully Ravine, it should be remembered, has been gorged into a deep ravine over time by the rains. In winter the sandy path turns back into a torrential river, flowing down to the sea.

Getting There

Arriving in Turkey by plane, there are two International airports that best serve you for getting to the Gallipoli region. These are Istanbul, where the *Atatürk Havalimani* Airport is situated about ten miles west of the city, and Izmir, where the *Adnan Menderes* Airport is about five miles outside the city. Istanbul, once called Constantinople, is a beautiful city, which contains many ancient historical sites and is also good for shopping in the bazaars. On the other hand, it is one of the worst cities to drive in, and the sooner it is left to get out on the open road the better. Izmir is not picturesque, and again should be left as

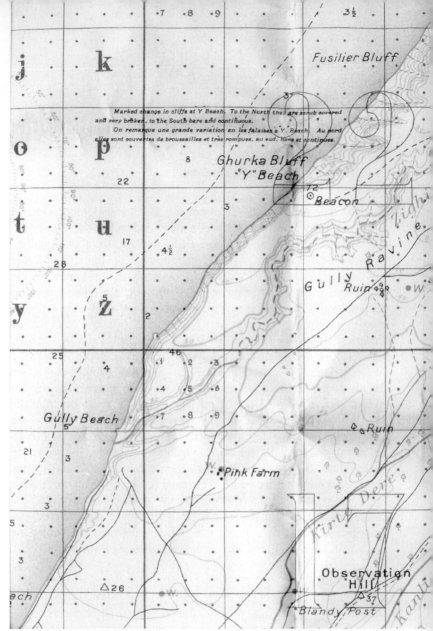

Map 2. Gully Ravine. (Reduced from the Turkish 1:5000 Survey)

soon as possible. Hiring a car is the best way to get to Gallipoli, costing about GBP 200 a week. Make sure the car has air conditioning for the summer months; it is definitely worth paying the extra. There is also a bus/coach service that can take you to the region very cheaply for about GBP 8, but the journey takes its time and can be very

18

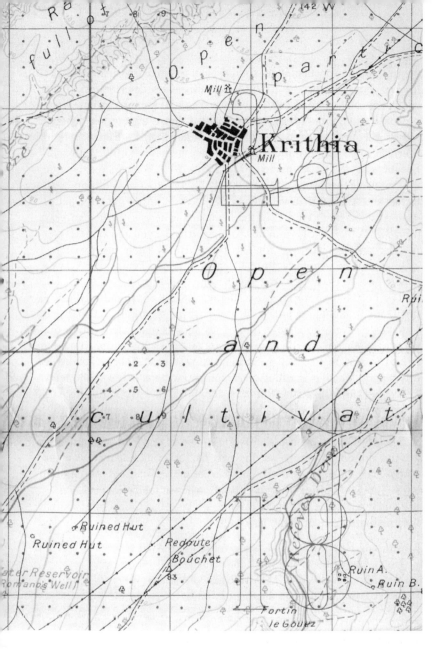

uncomfortable. Once there though, you will need your own transport. It is possible to hire a car or motorcycle, or use one of the small battlefield tour companies based in Eceabat or Canakkale.

The trip from either Istanbul or Izmir will take approximately 5 hours, totalling around 230 miles. Road conditions vary greatly, but the majority of the way is now on solid asphalt roads. There is a motorway for the first part of the journey, but this soon deteriorates to the equivalent of a B road, which can be rough, dodging the numerous potholes, crumbling edges, and the odd tortoise attempting a brave crossing. Follow the signs to Canakkale (Chanak in 1915) or Gelibolu (Turkish for Gallipoli), the town that gave its name to the Peninsula. Eceabat (had the Greek name of Maidos in 1915) is the major town on the Peninsula that also acts as a central hub for a tour of Gallipoli, with Helles and Anzac/Suvla very close. The nearest, if not the only, petrol station on the southern part of the Peninsula is here, as is the car ferry (*Feribot*). A pleasant 15-minute crossing will take you and vehicle over the Dardanelles 'narrows' for less than GBP 3. There are two ferry sailings that go regularly from Canakkale to the Peninsula. A large *feribot* goes to Eceabat, and a smaller one to Kilitbahir.

The hotels are not expensive, the equivalent of around GBP 20 a night, many including breakfast and an evening meal. Eceabat and Canakkale have a good selection of restaurants and cafes, eating out being very cheap. For the easiest access to Helles and Gully Ravine it is best to stay in Eceabat or Seddülbahir (Sedd el Bahr). Canakkale offers pretty much everything, although you will need to take the ferry every morning to cross the Narrows, and the drive will cut the time you could spend at Gallipoli by about two hours. I have previously stayed at both Hotel Eceabat and Pansiyon Helles Panorama, enjoying both immensely. Do not expect the luxuries that you may be accustomed to at other European hotels, as this part of Turkey is not really on the tourist map, the only visitors being the Gallipoli battlefield tourists and a few Turkish families who go to the beaches in the holiday season.

Check out some of the following, or visit the Canakkale Tourist Information Office near the Ferry terminal.

Canakkale Hotels
Hotel Akol – Tel: + 90 (286) 217 9456
Hotel Anafartala – Tel: +90 (286) 217 4454
Hotel Truva – Tel: + 90 (286) 217 1024
Anzac House – Tel: + 90 (286) 217 0156

Eceabat Hotels
Hotel Eceabat – Tel: +90 (286) 814 2458
Hotel Kum – Tel: +90 (286) 814 1455
TJ's Tours and Hostel – Tel: +90 (286) 814 3121
Hotel Ece – Tel: +90 (286) 814 1043

Seddülbahir Hotels
Pansiyon Helles Panorama – Tel: + 90 (286) 862 0035

Other Useful Addresses:

Canakkale Tourist Information Office
Iskele Meydani, 67
Canakkale
Tel: + 90 (286) 217 1187

TJ's Tours and Hostel
Kemlapasa Mah.
Cumhurriyet Cad.
No.5/A
17900 Eceabat
Tel +90 (286) 814 3121
Web site: www.anzacgallipolitours.com

Hassle Free Travel Agency
Cumhuriyet Meydani 61
Canakkale
Tel +90 (286) 213 5969

*Commonwealth War Graves
Commission*
2 Marlow Road,
Maidenhead,
Berkshire, SL6 7DX
Tel: +44 (0) 1628 634 221
Web site: www.cwgc.org.uk

*Commonwealth War Graves
Commission* (Canakkale Office)
Cimenlik Sohak,
Bagkur Ishani No.9,
Buro No.10
17001 Canakkale.
Tel +90 (286) 217 1010

Imperial War Museum
Lambeth Road,
London SE1 6HZ
Tel: +44 (0) 207 416 5000
Web site: www.iwm.org.uk

National Army Museum
Royal Hospital Road, Chelsea,
London SW3 4HT
Tel: +44 (0) 207 730 0717
Web site:
www.national-army-museum.ac.uk

Gallipoli Association
PO Box 26907,
London, SE21 8WB
Web site: www.gallipoli-association.org

The Gallipoli Association's key objectives are to keep alive the memory of the Gallipoli Campaign of 1915/16, in order to ensure that the men who fought and died in the campaign are not forgotten, and to encourage and facilitate the study of the campaign so that lasting benefit can be gained from its valuable lessons. An excellent journal called *The Gallipolian* is produced three times a year for members, and contains many articles and useful information. The association also runs visits to the Gallipoli battlefield.

Stephen Chambers, West Sussex, 2002.

THOSE HEROES THAT SHED THEIR BLOOD
AND LOST THEIR LIVES...
YOU ARE NOW LYING IN THE SOIL OF A FRIENDLY COUNTRY.
THEREFORE REST IN PEACE.
THERE IS NO DIFFERENCE BETWEEN THE JOHNNIES
AND THE MEHMETS TO US, WHERE THEY LIE SIDE BY SIDE
HERE IN THIS COUNTRY OF OURS...
YOU, THE MOTHERS
WHO SENT THEIR SONS FROM FAR AWAY COUNTRIES,

WIPE AWAY YOUR TEARS.
YOUR SONS ARE NOW LYING IN OUR BOSOM
AND ARE IN PEACE
AFTER HAVING LOST THEIR LIVES IN THIS LAND THEY HAVE
BECOME OUR SONS AS WELL.

Kemal Ataturk, 1934

1. Bartlett, E. Ashmead, *Despatches from the Dardanelles*, (1915), pp. 146-147
2. Creighton, Reverend Oswin, CF, *With the Twenty Ninth Division in Gallipoli: A Chaplain's Experience*, (1916), pp.136-137.
3. Behrend, Arthur, *Make me a Soldier- A Platoon Commander in Gallipoli*, (1961), p.105.

List of Maps

Chapter One

THE ADVANCE ON KRITHIA

A landing at Gully Beach, designated in April 1915 with the code Y2, was rejected as part of the original Helles landings because the mouth of the ravine was clearly heavily fortified. It was estimated that two platoons of 26/Infantry Regiment (9th Turkish Division) were stationed there. The closest landing points to Gully Ravine on 25 April 1915 were at Y Beach, which was totally undefended, and at X Beach, which had only a small picket of about twelve men. Y Beach was some 3,000 yards south west of Krithia, and was the nearest beach to the main objective of Achi Baba. It consisted of a narrow strip of beach at the foot of steep, thorny, scrub-covered cliffs about 150 feet high. On 25 April about 2,000 men of 1/Kings Own Scottish Borderers, the Plymouth Battalion Royal Marine Light Infantry and a company of 2/South Wales Borderers landed successfully with no opposition. Parties reconnoitred Gully Ravine and noted Krithia lying undefended. This force entrenched itself, awaiting the link-up from the other landings further south. Unknown to them, this would not take place owing to the heavy resistance met on the southern beaches. Also unknown at the time was the fact that this force was equal to the whole of the Turkish defence south of Achi Baba. The Turks eventually discovered the static force and threw repeated attacks at them from that afternoon and throughout the night. The landing was a

2/Royal Fusiliers in one of the small offshoot gullies, early May 1915.
(Croighton)

missed opportunity and tragically, owing to confusion, the troops withdrew early on 26 April.

On 27 April, with the Helles beachheads now consolidated, the weary and battered troops of the 29th Division could make their advance on Krithia and Achi Baba.[1] Around the beaches there was much congestion from the continuing landings of further troops, ammunition, stores, food and water. The men at this stage were becoming extremely fatigued from prolonged exertion and a lack of sleep that they had endured over the past couple of days. Fighting their way onto the beaches, repelling heavy Turkish counter-attacks, digging trenches, building encampments and bringing up supplies had begun to take their toll. The Turks, retiring back to Achi Baba, were in a similar situation, equally exhausted and in disarray. During the brilliant sunlight of the afternoon the general Allied advance met with little resistance. As dusk fell, the Allies had safely secured the toe of the Peninsula to a depth of about two miles, halting as night set in. This gave the troops some sense of further achievement, although the situation for the allies was still critical.

> *Blood, sweat, fire; with these we have forged our master key*
> *and forced it into the lock of the Hellespont, rusty and dusty with*
> *centuries of disuse.*[2]

The only opposition at this time was darkness and fatigue. Major-General Hunter-Weston now began the preparation for the final assault on the village of Krithia, and the heights of Achi Baba, both the fairly ambitious objectives for the first day of the landing.

The First Battle of Krithia

At 08:00, 28 April 1915, the First Battle of Krithia began with a fairly meagre bombardment. The 29th Division attacked on the Allied left, while the recently landed French 1st Division attacked on the right. Coming up against little Turkish resistance at first, mainly isolated snipers and the occasional shrapnel burst, they very soon met with more determined opposition from entrenched Turkish positions. 87 Brigade advanced on the left, their objective being Sari Tepe on the Aegean coast, and Yazy Tepe (Hill 472) at the end of Gully Ravine. 88 Brigade, in the middle, was to capture Krithia itself, whilst the French, on the right, were to link up at Kanli Dere with the British. This optimistic advance of over five miles was to be made by tired troops, using a complicated wheeling movement, against an unknown terrain and unknown enemy positions and with little artillery support.

1/Border Regiment and 1/Inniskilling Fusiliers were the first British

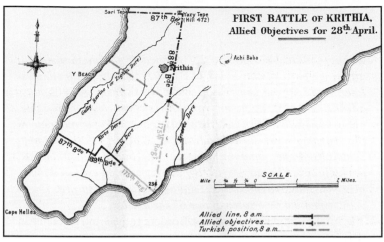

Map 3. First Battle of Krithia – Allied Objectives for 28 April 1915.

troops to reach the southern area of Gully Ravine, securing its mouth and Gully Beach with no resistance. The advance continued astride the ravine, with the Borders advancing along the bare strip of rocky ground that became known as Gully Spur, and the Inniskillings on the eastern side of the ravine along what became known as Fir Tree Spur. 2/South Wales Borderers were in reserve. But by mid-day, the advance had lost its early momentum; it was hopelessly disorganised and beginning to incur casualties. A Turkish strongpoint, near the abandoned Y Beach, put up heavy resistance that brought the advances along both spurs to a standstill. These tired invaders were not in a fit state to carry out an attack.

> Their vitality was at a low ebb, and the heat of the sun, combined with great shortage of water, was provoking an intolerable thirst.

Rhodes James writes of the Allied troops being:

> dead-tired, obeyed orders dumbly, some staggered around as though drugged, others just collapsed and slept where they fell.

Very few artillery pieces had been landed at this stage, and those that were only offered desultory support, and in many cases had to fire blind as the enemy's positions were not known. Naval gunfire did fill this gap, and offered critical support to the land forces during these early days. Off Y Beach, HMS *Queen Elizabeth* helped save the day in support of the tired Border Regiment who broke in the face of a Turkish counter-attack on Gully Spur. In Midshipman G.M.D. Maltby's journal he describes how the ship's guns literally annihilated a massed Turkish counter-attack, about a company strong:

> We weighed at 10.15 and steamed to 'Y' beach, opening fire almost immediately with our 6" (guns) on Turks in trenches

25

*amongst scrub. At 1.30 our 15" opened fire with shrapnel at
difference parts of cliff to left of Y beach ceasing fire 6 minutes
later. At 12.30 the Huns [sic] could be distinctly seen rapidly
advancing and firing from behind the farthest ridge. They came
along in huge numbers, and there being only a few of our men in
the advance trench to meet them. These fellers became
demoralized and many ran over the cliff, but the situation was
partially saved by our 15"(13,000 bullets), which exploded bang
over the Huns and those that it did not flatten out, turned. These
were wiped out by a salvo of our 6" shrapnel.*[4]

As the smoke and dust cleared, the Borders rallied and re-established
the line.

Not only had casualties taken their toll over the past couple of days,
weakening the 29th Division fighting order, but also ammunition, food
and water were becoming scarce. Many of the weary men had already
cast away their heavy packs; these contained not only extra
ammunition, but also 'iron rations' (The iron ration consisted of two
'hard-tack' biscuits, a tin of bully beef along with some tea and sugar).
The men had landed with two days' rations for 25th and 26th, and one
iron ration for the 27th. This iron ration was then ordered to last
another day, for those who still had one. The Zion Mule Corps[5] were
the only transport corps on Helles at this time, and were already
busying themselves by taking up vital supplies to the front. The
covered depths of Gully Ravine were becoming an ideal
communication path for movement of troops and supplies. The
commanding officer of the Zion Mule Corps, Lieutenant-Colonel J. H.
Patterson, recalls a night up the gully as:

*Shells from our own guns screamed and passed safely over the
ravine, but the shells from the Turkish batteries often burst exactly
overhead, scattering shrapnel all around, at other times plunking
into the cliff on our right and smothering us with clay and gravel.
The rattle of musketry was like the continuous roll of kettledrums,
and considering all our surroundings, and the fierce fight that
was going on, it was altogether a night to remember.*[6]

The new trench line above these depths was at this time literally just
the one, shallow, line with no support or reserve trenches. This was
held and consolidated by the troops as best they could. The First Battle
of Krithia was called off at 18:00 the same day. From the strategical
point of view, even though Krithia and Achi Baba still eluded capture,
it did enable the Allies to get firmly off the beaches and secure a much
deeper zone. This battle was to become typical of the whole campaign:

asking too much of the troops, with limited artillery, against strong entrenched enemy positions. The Allies had at this stage suffered 3,000 casualties out of 14,000 engaged in the battle; since 25 April, 400 officers and 8,500 men had been lost. No one had planned for or expected this. The shock and effect on morale on an army that had anticipated a walkover was shattering. Meanwhile Turkish strength, particularly in artillery, was growing rapidly.

The Turkish Night Counter-Attack

During the evening of 28 April a storm developed, drizzling rain adding to the already low morale of the troops. By the following morning the storm had died down, leaving the rest of the day and 30 April uneventful. This allowed the new line to be consolidated, the dead to be buried, the wounded tended and precious supplies brought up from the beaches. The lull before the next storm did not last long, as during the night of 1 May a huge and determined two division (9th and 7th) Turkish counter-attack was thrown against the allies, which continued throughout the night and the following morning. Out of the moonlit night a force estimated at about 10,000 strong attacked across the whole of the Helles front, crying 'Allah! Allah!', hitting both British and French lines hard:

> *The noise was deafening, they yelled and shouted like madmen, but above all the cry of 'Allah' could be heard...the battalion's right machine gun did considerable execution.*[7]

This night attack was a desperate effort to force the Allies back into the sea from the precious ground to which they were now clinging. Sergeant Dennis Moriarty, 1/Royal Munster Fusiliers, wrote in his diary:

The Turkish night attack. *The noise was deafening, they yelled and shouted like madmen, but above all the cry of 'Allah' could be heard...*

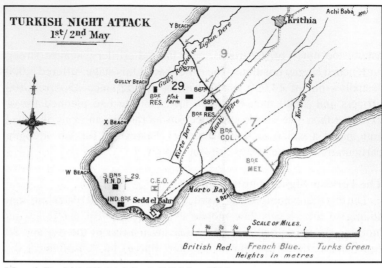

Map 4. Turkish Night Attack, 1/2 May 1915

About 5 p.m. enemy started a heavy shrapnel fire on our trenches...9 p.m. they started an attack, I am sure I will never forget that night as long as I live. They crept right up to our trenches (they were in thousands) and they made the night hideous with yells and shouting Allah, Allah. We could not help mowing them done. Some of them broke through in a part of our line but they never again got back as they were caught between the two lines of trenches. Some of the best men in the Regiment killed. When the Turks got to close quarters the devils used hand grenades and you could only recognise our dead by their Identity Discs.

My God, what a sight met us when day broke this morning. The whole ground in front was littered with dead Turks.

The ferocity of the Turkish attack did achieve several breakthroughs, including at Gully Ravine itself. Here the Turks broke through the first line of trenches, and came rushing down the ravine, only to be stopped by the fixed bayonets of 5/Royal Scots. Although the situation was serious, the defensive positions of the Allies proved that they could defeat these huge and determined counter-attacks. The Allies took the opportunity and made some counterattacks. 87 Brigade advanced 500 yards on the Allied left along Gully Spur, capturing the Turkish front line trench and quite a few prisoners. Unfortunately, 86 and 88 Brigades in the middle met stiff Turkish resistance, which compelled 87 Brigade to withdraw in the evening to straighten the line. By the end of the day, no significant advance had been made. The Turks tried another night attack on 3 May, mainly against the French, but this also failed. For the meantime, at least, until a new offensive could begin, the Allies' slender foothold on the Peninsula was retained.

The Second Battle of Krithia

Time was of the essence for an advance up the Peninsula, as the Turks were becoming stronger by the day. Reinforcements were arriving and the Turkish trenches were being strengthened. To renew the allied advance and secure the capture of Krithia and the Achi Baba Ridge, 125 (Lancashire Fusilier) Brigade from the 42nd Division, and 2 Australian Brigade and the New Zealand Brigade, from Anzac, were landed at Helles. 6 May saw the opening of the Second Battle of Krithia, an action that would involve three days continuous fighting. Attached to the depleted 29th Division were the newly arrived 125 Brigade and 29 Indian Brigade, which brought the Division's strength up to a full four brigades. The 29th Division had to break up 86 Brigade temporarily (4 May - 5 June) owing to its enormous casualties; the two Fusilier battalions were attached to 88 Brigade, and the Dubsters[9] to 87 Brigade.

Hunter-Weston's plans for the Gully Ravine area in this attack were basically the same as the first battle: to capture Yazy Tepe (Hill 472), Sari Tepe on the coast, and Achi Baba. Along Gully Spur the 6/Lancashire Fusiliers led 125 Brigade's attack, leaving 87 Brigade and

The bare plateau above Y Beach. Even though this photograph was taken later on in the campaign, when it became an Advanced Dressing Station, it shows clearly the open field of fire the Turkish had when their strongpoint was positioned here. (IWM Q13314)

The same view today. (© Chambers)

A contemporary drawing of the view from Y Beach, looking towards Lancashire Landing.

88 Brigade to attack along Fir Tree Spur and the centre whilst the French attacked over on the eastern side. The supporting artillery bombardment was virtually non-existent, to the extent that a Turkish staff officer actually reported that the British attacked on that day with no artillery preparations. The Turks at this stage had begun to reinforce their positions with machine-guns and wire. Prolonged trench warfare and the danger of a stalemate were fast becoming serious obstacles. Hamilton wrote in his diary that:

> ...the War Office urge me to throw my brave troops yet once more against machine guns in redoubts; to do it on the cheap; to do it without asking for the shells that give the attack a sporting chance.[10]

Turkish rifle, machine-gun and shellfire held up the advances almost immediately. The most severe fighting took place on Gully Spur, where Hunter-Weston, with visions of battlefield romanticism and gallant sacrifice, noted that 125 Brigade was 'blooded today'. The 6/Lancashire Fusiliers, with the 7/Lancashire Fusiliers in support, reached the bare plateau above Y Beach, but came up against the same Turkish strongpoint whose machine guns halted the 28 April attack. From this prominent bluff, above the shoreline cliffs, the Turks overlooked any British advance in the area.

The following is a poem by Corporal Edwin Bowker, Gordon Highlanders, who wrote of the Lancashire Fusilier attack that May.

> The gallant Lancashire Fusiliers are steady on parade,
> Against the Turks they did advance, a noble charge they made;
> With dauntless hearts they faced the foe, alas, 'tis sad to tell,
> In the fight for God and Right many a hero fell.
>
> For dash and style, the rank and file, amid the cannon's roar,
> Did never flinch nor yield an inch, but many are no more;
> Our heartfelt sympathy goes out to all who mourn the day,
> For loved ones who have gone before, in battle passed away.
>
> A roll of honour then prepare, and every name put on,
> That we may ever think of them although from earth they're gone,
> Success unto our allies brave, who never shrink or fear,
> To memory dear, the silent tear, for the Lancashire Fusilier.

This key position was, unfortunately, abandoned on the 26 April with the Y Force evacuation and now became a thorn in the British side. The

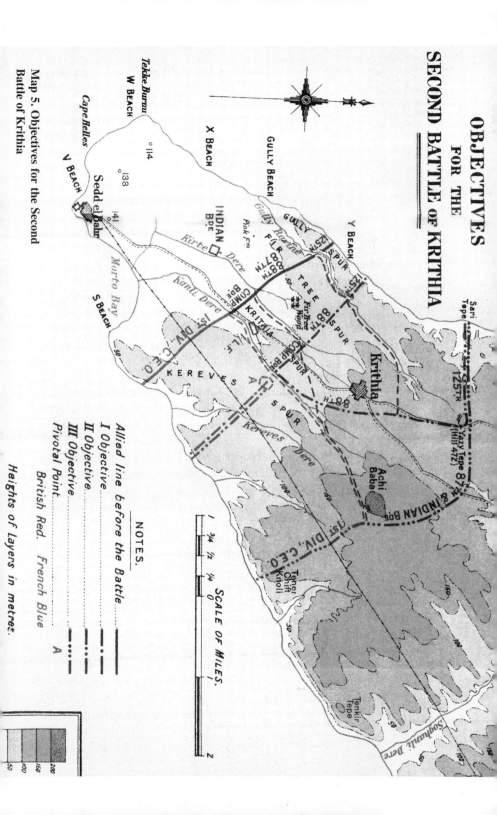

OBJECTIVES FOR THE SECOND BATTLE OF KRITHIA

NOTES.

Allied line before the Battle	
I Objective	
II Objective	
III Objective	
Pivotal Point	A
British Red. French Blue	

Heights of Layers in metres.

SCALE OF MILES.

Map 5. Objectives for the Second
Battle of Krithia

Bluff strongpoint was positioned on the southern bank of the steep scrubby nullah (a water channel, either dry or wet) that later became known as Gurkha Ravine. It dominated the area some 300 feet high up above Y Beach, and about 500 yards northeast of the British trenches. Since the landing the Turks had converted it into a powerful fortress, estimated to contain five machine guns. Reinforcements could make no further progress and the supporting ship, HMS *Sapphire*, could not locate its position. The following day, 7 May, HMS *Swiftsure*, HMS *Talbot* and a balloon ship named *Manica* were sent to locate and destroy the strongpoint. This visit also proved unsuccessful, and further troop advances only enticed the Turks guns to fire to murderous affect. Repeated efforts by the Lancashire Fusiliers to get forward all failed. Hamilton wrote:

> They are faced by a horrid redoubt held by machine guns, and they are to rush it with the bayonet. It is a high thing to ask of Territorials but against an enemy who is fighting for his life, and for the existence of his country, we have to call upon every one for efforts, which, under any other conditions, might be considered beyond their strength.[11]

Supported by 87 Brigade, a party of the KOSB tried moving under the cliffs, whilst a party of the Inniskillings moved up Gully Ravine in an effort to help the Lancashire Territorials. Even HMS *Queen Elizabeth* arrived off Y Beach to add her powerful guns to the demolishing of the cliff area in hope of destroying this position. Every advance or show of movement was met again and again by the Turkish machine-guns. By nightfall on 7 May the situation on the spur remained unchanged.

Second Lieutenant Terence Verschoyle, 5/Royal Inniskilling Fusiliers and Brigade liaison officer to the 6/Lancashire Fusiliers, recounted events on 7 May 1915, whilst holding a newly captured trench:

> Bullets were hitting the parapets of trenches as though they were the butts on a rifle range. The trench was the one captured by the 6th Fus. [6/Lancashire Fusiliers] the previous day. It was not very deep and was full of men from each battalion of the Brigade. One could hardly move about as it was so shallow...I don't think anyone had seen any enemy except some dead ones, I hadn't and all I knew was that plenty of bullets were coming from our front where there was an amount of scrub and bushes.

And with the word to advance:

> I with some others got out and started to run forward. The whizz of bullets was terrific and one knew it was impossible not to be hit within seconds. The only thing to do was to lie down.

Bullets were hitting the trench we had just left and cutting the grass round about. I got my entrenching tool out of its sheath and held that and my rifle butt in front of my head. Possibly they might have stopped a bullet...[12]

On the other side of Gully Ravine an advance was concentrated on Fir Tree Spur, the action here becoming known as the battle of Fir Tree Wood. Fir Tree Wood, from which the ridge got its name, was a scattered wood of fir trees along the downward slope of this ridge, to the left of a dry creek-bed. Towards its middle was a small cultivated field, devoid of any cover and carpeted by a rich growth of white daisies, interspersed with red poppies, known as the Daisy Patch or Daisy Field. The Turks, with at least two machine guns, held the wood and many snipers hid in the growth ready to pour fire into any advancing troops. The open field of fire enabled them to wreak destruction among the advancing troops, the machine guns sweeping the ground like a hose, firing at any movement, near or far. The 5/Royal Scots attacked the wood at 10:00 that morning and were able to secure a footing, which turned out to be a death trap, on its southern fringe. What they discovered was a wood full of snipers, body and rifle painted green, camouflaged with twigs and branches from the trees, so much so that they resembled trees and bushes. Heavy casualties were suffered by the Scots whilst attempting to take the wood, but after numerous acts of bravery the Royal Scots were forced to withdraw. At 17:00 the 1/Essex, 1/Borders and the Dubsters attacked the wood, managing to advance as far as 300 yards into it. Unfortunately after

Map 6. Second Battle of Krithia, 6 – 8 May 1915

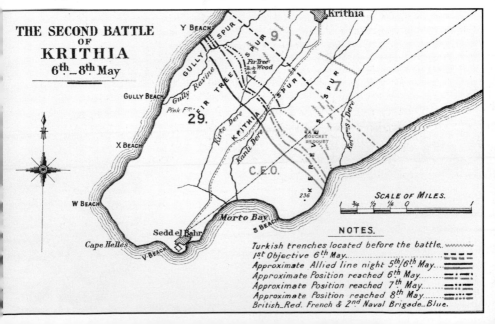

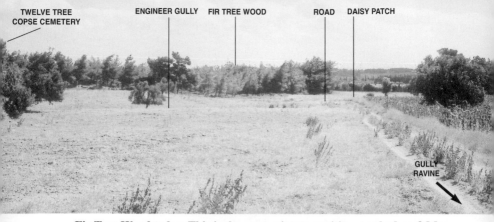

TWELVE TREE
COPSE CEMETERY

ENGINEER GULLY   FIR TREE WOOD

ROAD   DAISY PATCH

GULLY
RAVINE

Fir Tree Wood today. This is the approximate position reached on 8 May.
(© Chambers)

three determined advances into the wood, all were driven out with heavy casualties. Part of the Turkish defence of this area was formed by accurate and persistent enfilade fire that came over the ravine from Gully Spur. The Bluff strongpoint, mentioned earlier, not only seriously hampered any further advances on Gully Spur, but also helped to frustrate the Fir Tree Spur attacks.

On Friday 7 May Reverend Oswin Creighton, Chaplain to 86 Brigade wrote:

> *I went along the West Krithia road, past the Pink Farm, and then into a deep gully leading towards the firing line. When I had got the horses down into it, I left them with the groom and started to walk up the gully. On the way I met K-, who had just left the*

The gully road leading through the ravine, early May 1915. *When I had got the horses down into it, I left them with the groom and started to walk up the gully.* (IWM Q14847)

Munsters. They had not been in the thick of the fighting, but a good deal of shooting was still going on. Stray bullets were whistling about, and some went uncomfortably close. However, I wanted to get up if possible, until one or two came so close I decided it would be wiser to return.

...I left the horses and made my way onto Gully Beach where the 87th Field Ambulance is, but found no chance of getting up to the regiments. A very deep gully runs down to Gully Beach, but it was said to be full of snipers.

The road drops into the gully, which is very deep and narrow and goes all the way up to the bed of the stream, winding along through steep banks covered with scrubby bushes and quantities of flowers. They are making the road gradually, and it is a regular highway. All the time the 'ping, ping' of bullets overhead. I am always a little suspicious of the stray bullets, which have a way of dropping into the gully.[13]

Second Lieutenant T. Verschoyle recalls the situation ten days after the landings. It could be argued that it was safer to be in the front line than behind the lines in the support trenches and on the beaches, which were constantly being shelled. A major danger at Gallipoli was being preyed upon in what became the snipers' playground:

...there were still snipers in our territory behind the front line and of course everyone was on the qui vive for these gentry for one felt that one might get a bullet out of the blue any moment. They hid in trees, bushes or holes dug in the ground and in some cases had no rations for a week or more. They were brave men because when discovered their day's work in the world was over! On our way up to the high ground between the gully and the sea we thought we were sniped at because quite a few shots rang out.[14]

There are many accounts of casualties by snipers. Although in many instances this was probably true, it was sometimes the stray bullet, not the sniper that took its victim. With tensions high on both sides, bullets would often be whizzing in both directions.

On the lovely spring morning of 8 May, two brigades of Australian and New Zealanders, which had been transferred earlier from ANZAC, came into the action.[15] The four battalions of New Zealanders[16] were to have their own taste of the Daisy Patch. Their attack made little progress, with only light elements of the force getting as far as the wood. Heavy fire from the wood, and the enfilade fire from the machine guns on Gully Spur, checked any advance. The New

TWELVE TREE COPSE CEMETERY

FIR TREE WOOD & SPUR

Panoramic view of the Krithia Spur, where the Australian Brigade went to their Balaclava. (© Chambers)

Zealanders were forced to retire over the open area, leaving their dead and dying amongst the carpet of poppies and daisies. This gallant attack in the killing ground of the Daisy Patch failed to achieve any success, most of the troops not even reaching or seeing the Turkish frontline. There were nearly 800 casualties out of just over two and a half thousand men involved in the attack. Later in the day, as the heat of the morning battle died down, on the New Zealanders' right, the Australian Brigade[17], bayonets fixed, made its own magnificent charge. Over the open ground on Krithia Spur, their advance of almost a thousand yards was met immediately with Turkish bullets and shellfire. Many of the Australians did not even reach the British front line, let alone the Turkish. Only an hour before, the Australians had been resting behind the lines; now they had lost 1,000 men, a third of their number, in a matter of minutes. Like the New Zealand attack, this too collapsed like a pack of playing cards, 'two senseless and avoidable Balaclavas'[18]. Neither party reached the Turkish frontline, many of the men not even seeing a Turk.

87 Brigade was ordered to renew the attack on the Bluff strongpoint above Y Ravine, and then to push on to the trenches west of Krithia. HMS *Queen Elizabeth*, *Sapphire* and *Dublin* all tried to destroy the redoubt with their guns, but failed as in previous attempts. An artillery bombardment of sorts opened at 17:30, which was followed ten minutes later by an assault by the South Wales Borderers. Unfortunately, as soon as the meagre barrage lifted, the Borderers were immediately met with devastating shrapnel and machine-gun fire:

Numbers fell, especially in the second line, which was mown down wholesale as it crossed the parapet.[19]

As soon as it became obvious that the first waves were being held up, still a hundred yards short of the Turkish trenches, the attack was called off to save further waste of life. Not a single yard was gained. Two further gallant attempts to take the mound were made by the Dubsters early on 9 May, but both ended in failure. It was now clear that without

the capture of this post all further advances in this area would be futile. The battered ruins of Krithia were left eluding the British grasp once again.

The second battle of Krithia had now come to an official end. After three days of fighting in the brilliant sunshine the Turkish line had not yet been reached or even seen by most of the troops. Amazingly, between 6 – 8 May the Turks were unaware that there was actually a full-scale attack taking place. The accurate Turkish machine-gun, sniper and shellfire, from their positions higher up on the ridge, could observe and check any troop movement that came into the open, stopping dead the Allied advance. However, the determination and dogged valour of the British assault stretched the Turks to the limit, and on occasion the assault almost achieved the required breakthrough. The majority of the British troops were killed before they even reached their own support lines, let alone the front line. All that could be done

Australian stretcher-bearers in Gully Ravine, near the path that leads up into the Eski lines. (IWM Q14848)

by 9 May was to consolidate the position reached so far. A small gain of 200 yards on Gully Spur and about 400 yards along Fir Tree Spur was all that was achieved, and this position was still half a mile short of Hunter-Weston's objective for 25 April. Allied casualties were mounting; 6,500 casualties, about thirty percent of the troops engaged, had been taken for an advance of only 600 yards. Aspinall-Oglander commented:

> the Great War furnishes few examples of a series of offensive operations being entered upon with troops so worn out by continuous fighting and lack of sleep as those who took part in the Second Battle of Krithia.[20]

The troops on both sides were utterly exhausted, and low on artillery ammunition, especially the British:

> We are now on our last legs. The beautiful Battalions of the 25th April are wasted skeletons now; shadows of what they had been,[21]

Artillery stocks were seriously depleted, with hardly a shell left in the reserve dumps. Extra ammunition was on its way, but this would take at least two weeks to arrive. Even though there were not enough shells left for another major offensive, the British kept the pressure on the Turks during the rest of May by a series of 'stealthy and almost bloodless advances'.[22] This bite-and-hold tactic succeeded in gaining more ground than Second Krithia, bringing the opposing front lines a lot closer together. Unfortunately the lessons were not learned, as the Third Battle of Krithia would later prove.

The Gurkhas take the Bluff

By 11 May Brigadier-General Vaughan Cox's 29 Indian Brigade had taken over the Gully Spur sector from 86 Brigade, who came out of the line with the whole of the 29th Division for a hard-earned rest. The day earlier he had 6/Gurkha reconnoitre the Turkish Bluff strongpoint in order to plan a fresh attack, which was scheduled for the afternoon of 12 May.

Wednesday, 12 May, began wet, with the rain falling non-stop until about 10:00. This was the first rain experienced by the troops since the landings, and it was fairly welcome too. At 15:30 two batteries of the Royal Field Artillery, which were at the disposal of 6/Gurkha, began shelling the Bluff. This continued until dusk, when 89/Punjabis, on the right hand side of the ravine, with rifle and machine gun, and the artillery with shell, opened a heavy fire on the Turkish 'H' trenches on Fir Tree Spur. This was a ruse to turn the Turks attention away from the Bluff on Gully Spur.

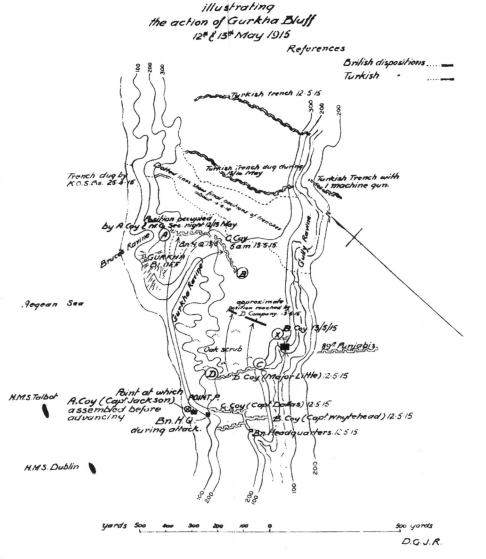

Map 7. The Action at Gurkha Bluff, 12/13 May 1915

Note: On British trench maps for Gallipoli all the Turkish trenches were prefixed with a letter. From the eastern section of the Peninsula the F trenches were at Kanli Dere (Achi Baba Nullah); the G trenches were west of Kanli Dere to Kirte Dere (Krithia Nullah). Those on Fir Tree Spur, east of Gully Ravine, had H prefixes; and those west of Gully Ravine on Gully Spur had J prefixes.

The Gallipoli campaign suffered from poor topographical

intelligence and allegedly inadequate and inaccurate maps. Many of the maps used in the early days of the campaign were legacies from the Crimean War or obsolete Turkish sources, all unreliable. Before the landings, ground survey was impossible, and there was a lack of suitable aircraft, photographic equipment and trained observers. Limited reconnaissances were made from the naval ships, mostly after the landings, and towards the closure of the campaign the quality of trench maps had greatly improved.

Whilst the bombardment was in progress, 'A' Company, 6/Gurkha, under Captain D. Jackson, began to move quietly, under the cover of darkness, down onto the beach and along the shoreline to the foot of the Bluff. The bombardment was joined by the guns of HMS *Talbot* and HMS *Dublin*, who concentrated their efforts in pulverizing the Bluff with their high explosives. The ravine by the Bluff, then known as Y Gully (later to become known as Gurkha Ravine), was understood to be covered by a Turkish machine gun, so extra attention was given to this area as the bombardment continued.

By 20:00 'A' Company had covertly scaled Y Gully, and upon reaching the top found to their utter astonishment that no Turks were there to defend the position. Immediately the area was consolidated, and reinforcements brought up. Why this area was evacuated nobody really knows. Possibly the exposure of the position from the sea, which left it open to naval fire, or the threat of being outflanked, had influenced the Turkish withdrawal. Anyhow, the Turks had fled, leaving the position in the hands of the British, where it would remain until the evacuation. This well-planned and executed assault contrasts sharply

Map 8. Sketch of Gurkha Bluff Trenches held by 29 Indian Brigade

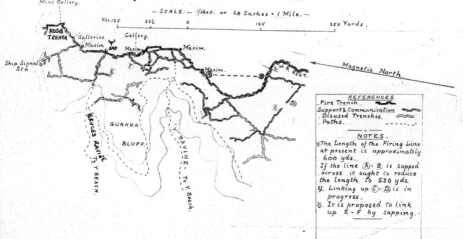

with the futile frontal attacks made only a few days earlier.

At 04:00 on the morning of the 13 May Captain J. S. Dallas had reinforced this position with his 'C' Company. At that precise time the enemy, realising their mistake, counter-attacked the Bluff in force, only to be met by the Gurkhas heavy and accurate small-arms fire and the supporting Royal Field Artillery (RFA) guns.

With this counter-attack successfully beaten back, another problem arose. There still lay about a 300-yard gap between the Bluff and Gully Ravine. To fully consolidate the newly captured ground, the line needed to be immediately joined up with the positions at Gully Ravine. At 06:30 Major W. Campbell-Little's 'D' Company attempted to advance across the scrub from the old frontline but very quickly came under very heavy Turkish fire. Unable to advance any further, they dug in, and a rough line was established from the gully to where Captain H. R. Whytehead's 'B' Company had begun sapping towards them. At this stage no connection could be made with 'A' and 'C' Companies over on the Bluff, who were left isolated covering the extreme British left. Reinforcements from two companies of the 14/Sikhs and the 1/Inniskilling Fusiliers were brought up. During the day and late afternoon the Turks kept up a heavy fire, but no counter-attack ever developed. The period ended successfully with the capture of the Bluff and nearly 500 yards of the coastline, and 150 yards along the left bank

Gurkha Bluff today. (© Chambers)

A Gurkha standing on Y Beach (Gurkha Beach) shortly after the capture of Gurkha Bluff. (© Chambers)

of Gully Ravine. The casualties were light: both Major Campbell-Little and Captain Dallas were severely wounded, with eighteen other ranks killed and another thirty-nine wounded.

On 17 May, General Routine Order No.160 was published:

> *In order to mark the good work done by the 1/6th Gurkha Rifles in capturing the Bluff on the coast west of Krithia, the General Officer Commanding has ordered that this Bluff will in future be known as 'Gurkha Bluff.' This name will be added to those mentioned in General Routine Order No.101, dated May 2nd, 1915.*

The ravine on its northern side became known as 'Bruce's Ravine', named after Lieutenant-Colonel the Hon. Charles Granville Bruce, the commander of the 6/Gurkha Rifles. The ravine to the south side of Y Ravine was known as Gurkha Ravine.

With one complication out of the way, another developed on 15 May. The 69/Punjabis and 89/Punjabis had to be withdrawn from Gallipoli, and were ordered to prepare for embarkation to Egypt. They later arrived on the Western Front in June 1915. The reason for withdrawing these two battalions from the Peninsula was that it was not considered

Lieutenant-Colonel C. G. Bruce, Commanding Officer, 6/Gurkha Rifles. Bruce was later severely wounded during the Battle of Gully Ravine and evacuated in July 1915.

6/Gurkhas in a trench. The man in the background has a Hypo helmet gas mask bag around his neck. These began to be issued at Gallipoli during June 1915.

desirable to employ Mohammedan troops against the Turks. Major Allanson, who later commanded 6/Gurkha, noted in his diary that the two Punjabi regiments, each containing two Muslim companies, had earlier sent in a petition not to fight against their fellow Muslims, the Turks. Though these regiments had already shown themselves to be brave fighters, Brigadier-General Cox could not afford to have them in the line as the risk was too great. Both battalions were replaced in early June by two further Gurkha regiments, 5/Gurkha and 10/Gurkha Rifles.

KOSB Trench

The positions during the next few days were strengthened and pushed forward to within 80 to 100 yards of the Turkish trenches. On 20 May the 1/Inniskilling Fusiliers managed to advance the line considerably on the extreme left, by Gurkha Bluff. Lying a little further out to the north of the Gurkha Bluff, in No Man's Land, were the old trenches dug by the 1/King's Own Scottish Borderers during the Y Beach landings on 25 April. These were later abandoned during the tragic and unnecessary withdrawal the following day. During the evening, elements of 6/Gurkha, under Captain Hugh Whytehead, had pushed forward and occupied this trench, known as KOSB Trench, consolidating it into the new British line. The Gurkhas handed over the position to the Inniskillings the following day, leaving behind a Maxim gun for their support.

At 14:30 on 22 May, barely half an hour after HMS *Talbot* was withdrawn from support on the left flank position because, of a

43

submarine scare,[23] the Turks attacked, cleverly taking full advantage of the situation. Both the KOSB Trench and a T-Sap that had begun to be dug out from the newly constructed British line were captured, along with the Gurkha Maxim. Elements of the Turkish attacking force also got as far as the second line, but were very quickly shot down. At about 16:00 the Gurkhas counter-attacked, forcing the Turks back after a stubborn fight with kukri and bayonet. Both KOSB Trench and the Maxim gun were recaptured, but at the loss of Captain Whytehead:

> The K.O.S.B. Trench was a mass of dead, British and Turks; the parapet, partly due to the efforts of the enemy to convert the trench to their own use, and partly on account of the scuffle in the trench, practically ceased to exist, It was therefore filled in, and the occupants withdrew to the old firing line 100 yards in the rear.[24]

Captain Hugh Richard Augustin Whytehead, 6/Gurkha Rifles, was killed in the attack on KOSB Trench on 22 May 1915, aged thirty-four. He had previously served in the Boer War, transferring from the Northumberland Fusiliers to the Indian Army in 1903:

> From the day he joined his time was devoted to the interests of the Regiment. As Quartermaster, and later as Adjutant, he was untiring in his efforts to promote efficiency, whilst a more conscientious worker would be difficult to find. He was buried next day immediately above Y Beach on the south-west side of Gurkha Ravine. [25]

After the war his grave could not be positively identified by the Imperial (later Commonwealth) War Graves Commission. He is commemorated today on Special Memorial C.456 in Twelve Tree Copse.

Captain H. R. A. Whytehead, 6/Gurkha Rifles. He was killed during the recapture of KOSB trench. (© Chambers)

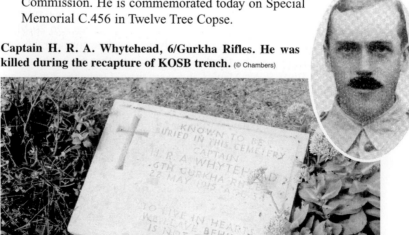

T-Sap also saw some determined and fierce fighting that day, where the Inniskillings managed to recapture the post from the Turks. The following day, 23 May, the Turks again moved up to try and occupy the now abandoned and filled-in KOSB Trench. They were quickly driven off by the Inniskillings who, later on with the help of the Gurkhas, began to re-dig the trench and once again link it with the British line.

An early view of Y Ravine soon after its capture.

The Heavens open

During the evening of Tuesday 25 May the darkened clouds suddenly opened to release a torrential downpour. Reverend Creighton, who went into the gully that day to take a funeral for a Royal Fusilier man shot through the head earlier, wrote:

> There had been a tremendous pour of rain the night before in the gully, though not a drop had fallen on the beach. The water had washed away a good deal of the road they had made up the gully, and the trenches were almost impassable, so they had been walking along the top when this man happened to be hit.[26]

Lieutenant Arthur Behrend, 4/East Lancashire Regiment, who was marching with his men up the gully, gives a graphic description of that day:

> At half-past five, while we were still tramping wearily along the stream bed towards the firing line, the sky clouded darkly and a few heavy drops splashed down. Then came the deluge. The rain descended in sheets and within a couple of minutes the dry stream bed was awash and ankle deep. We all scuttled for what little shelter there was; with Stancliffe and Heaps I took refuge under a ledge of overhanging cliff. I had already pulled my waterproof sheet over my head, and at first it kept me dry. But chunks of earth came tumbling down on us once the rain had saturated the cliff above our heads, and finally our shelter collapsed and we found ourselves standing beneath what is aptly known in Westmorland as a spout...it was then I touched the lowest-yet depths of misery.[27]

The rains began to wash away parts of the cliff, turning the bottom of the ravine into a torrent of muddy water thundering down towards the sea. The stream bed quickly rose, causing the floodwaters to carry with it all kinds of equipment, trees, animals and even dead bodies, washed out of their shallow graves.

The following morning after the rains had stopped Behrend goes on to write:

> *The sun was beginning to creep down the sides of the Gully, and I undressed and spread all my clothes on the scrub to dry. An hour later every man in the company was doing the same, and the cliff side looked like a vast laundry. By ten o'clock the whole Gully was bathed in hot sunlight; we wriggled and squirmed like dogs in the lovely warmth and our drying clothes began to steam, a sight which appealed to the men's sense of humour. By eleven the heat had become unbearable.*[28]

Mud and mule after a heavy downpour. (IWM Q13650)

'A Stretcher Bearer's Poem' by Jack Todd

Tramping up the gully,
Tramping up the gully,
With your stretcher every day and night,
While shrapnel overhead is zipping
And bullets all around are pipping,
When your feet are weary and you're far from cheery,
And you seem to know quite well,
You're going,
You're going,
Tramping up the gully,
Tramping up the gully,
That will lead you to the gates of hell.

1. The 700 foot hill was known to the Turks as Alchi Tepe, but to the British as Achi Baba, a result of a map error. The British troops also referred to it as 'Archie Barber' or 'Archibald'. Today it is called Alçi Tepe (Plaster Hill), sharing the same name as the village of Krithia, called today Alcitepe.
2. Hamilton, Sir Ian, *Gallipoli Diary*, (1920), Vol.I, p.158.
3. Rhodes James, Robert, *Gallipoli*, (1965), p.141.
4. Midshipman G. M.D. Maltby's papers are in a private collection.
5. Mainly consisting of Russian Jewish volunteers who had fled Palestine on the outbreak of war with Turkey.
6. Patterson, Lieutenant-Colonel J. H, *With the Zionists in Gallipoli*, (1916), pp.116-117.
7. Atkinson, C. T, *The History of the South Wales Borderers 1914-1918*, (1931), p.114.
8. 29 Indian Brigade landed on 1 May and consisted of 6/Gurhkas, 14/Sikhs, 69/Punjabis and 89/Punjabis. 125 (Lancashire Fusilier) Brigade landed on 5 May and consisted of 5/Lancashire Fusiliers, 6/Lancashire Fusiliers, 7/Lancashire Fusiliers and 8/Lancashire Fusiliers.
9. The 'Dubster Battalion' was the temporary amalgamation of the Royal Dublin Fusiliers and Royal Munster Fusiliers made after the heavy casualties they suffered during the V Beach landings. On 19 May they resumed as separate units.
10. Hamilton, *Op.Cit.*, (1920), Vol.I, p.198.
11. Ibid., p.208.
12. Verschoyle, T, *My Gallipoli Story*, from *Gallipolian* No.48, Summer 1985, p.36.
13. Creighton, Reverend Oswin, CF, *With the Twenty Ninth Division in Gallipoli: A Chaplain's Experience*, (1916), pp.80-82.
14. Verschoyle, Op.Cit., p.34.
15. The New Zealand Brigade and 2 Australian Brigade landed at Cape Helles on the night of 5 May, returning to Anzac on 19 May.
16. The New Zealand Brigade comprised of the Wellington, Auckland, Canterbury and Otago Battalions.
17. 2 Australian Brigade comprised of 5, 6, 7 and 8 Australian (Victoria) Battalions.
18. Pugsley, Christopher, *Gallipoli, The New Zealand Story*, (1984), p.18.
19. Atkinson, *Op.Cit.*, (1931), p.116.
20. Aspinall-Oglander, Brigadier-General C. F, *History of the Great War, Military Operations: Gallipoli*, Vol.I, (1929), p.333.
21. Hamilton, *Op.Cit.*, (1920), p.209.
22. Rhodes James, Robert, *Gallipoli*, (1965), p.209.
23. There was due concern as HMS *Goliath* had already been sunk on 17 May in Morto Bay. Two further capital ships were sunk in May; HMS *Triumph* on 24 May (off Anzac) and HMS *Majestic* (off W Beach) on 27 May.
24. Ryan, D. G. J, *Historical Record of the 6th Gurkha Rifles*, (1925), p.93.
25. Ibid., p.94.
26. Creighton, Reverend Oswin, CF, *With the Twenty Ninth Division in Gallipoli: A Chaplain's Experience*, (1916), pp.111-112.
27. Behrend, Arthur, *Make me a Soldier- A Platoon Commander in Gallipoli*, (1961), p.106.
28. Ibid., p.111.

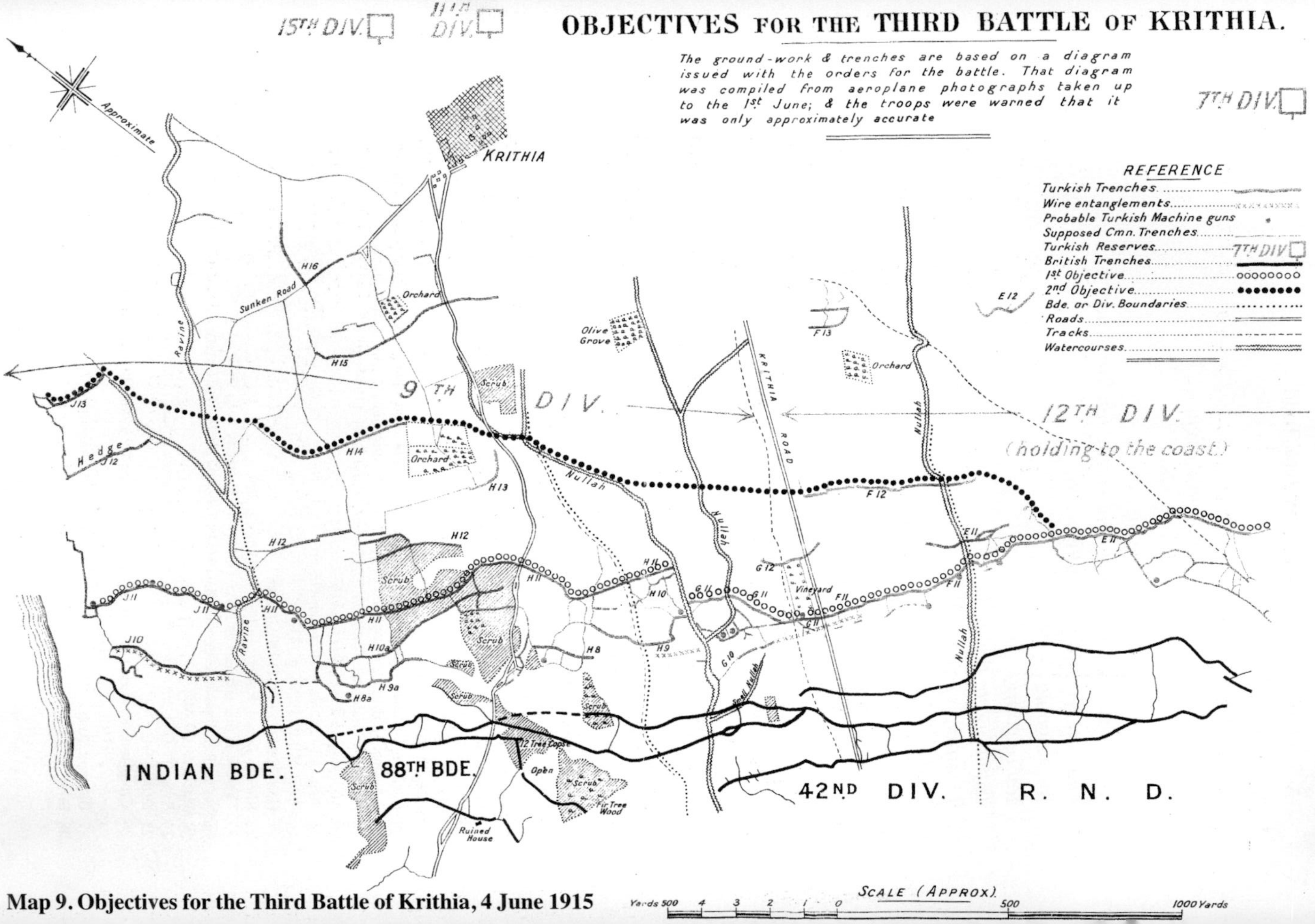

OBJECTIVES FOR THE THIRD BATTLE OF KRITHIA.

The ground-work & trenches are based on a diagram issued with the orders for the battle. That diagram was compiled from aeroplane photographs taken up to the 1st June; & the troops were warned that it was only approximately accurate

REFERENCE

Turkish Trenches...........	
Wire entanglements........	
Probable Turkish Machine guns	
Supposed Cmn. Trenches....	
Turkish Reserves.	•
British Trenches...........	ooooooooo
1st Objective.	●●●●●●●
2nd Objective.	●●●●●●
Bde. or Div. Boundaries.	
Roads.	
Tracks.	
Watercourses.	

15TH DIV.   H.Q. DIV.   7TH DIV.

KRITHIA

9TH DIV.

12TH DIV.
(holding to the coast.)

42ND DIV.   R. N. D.

88TH BDE.

INDIAN BDE.

KRITHIA ROAD

Approximate

SCALE (APPROX)

1000 Yards

500

Yards 500   0   1   2   3   4   Yards 500

Map 9. Objectives for the Third Battle of Krithia, 4 June 1915

Chapter Two

THE VALLEY OF DEATH – THE BATTLE OF THE FOURTH OF JUNE

Hunter-Weston, now commanding the newly formed VIII Corps, had been busily planning another offensive to include over 30,000 men and, now that there were adequate shell supplies on the Peninsula, a heavy artillery barrage. Instead of setting objectives that were vague and grandiose in ambition, the advance would be limited to about 800 yards.

At 08:00 on 4 June the British bombardment begun, pounding the Turkish lines continuously until 10:30. Following a half hour break, to give the Turks the idea that an attack was coming so as to catch them in the open, the barrage re-commenced. This *ruse de guerre* achieved its aim, as the Turks quickly prepared for an attack that did not materialise, only to be met with the second instalment of artillery as the bombardment reopened at 11:00. This lasted for another twenty minutes, and then ceased. The British troops in the front line fixed bayonets and opened rapid fire on the Turkish trenches, in another ruse to get the Turks to man their trenches, and again they were delivered another artillery instalment. For this attack, the 29th Division, 42nd Division, Royal Naval Division and also the 1st and 2nd French Divisions were made ready along the whole of the Helles front. The Turkish 9th Division held the line from the Aegean and Gully Ravine through to the Krithia Road, where the Turkish 12th Division continued the line through to the Dardanelles. During this second lull, however, it was noticed that on Gully Spur the artillery had not destroyed the barbed wire in front of J.9 trench, the majority of it being intact. Nothing could be done at this time, and at 11:30 the artillery continued the bombardment, finally stopping at 12:00 when the infantry went over the top, into a brilliant summer's day, to meet their fate.

29 Indian Brigade formed the Allied left in this attack, with 1/Lancashire Fusiliers attached from 86 Brigade in order to compensate the loss of both Punjabi Battalions. The 14/Sikhs attacked up Gully Ravine, whilst the Lancashire Fusiliers attacked in the open along Gully Spur, against J.10, leaving 6/Gurkha to make their advance along the cliffs. With little artillery and no howitzer support these units were all brought to a standstill in front of the uncut Turkish wire, taking heavy casualties from the intense rifle and machine-gun fire thrown at

them from the Turkish trenches. The Lancashire Fusiliers were cut down almost immediately upon leaving their trenches. One of the few who reached the Turkish wire was Captain Harold Robert Clayton, who was commanding 'D' Company. Clayton, a veteran of the W Beach Landings, who showed great bravery during that action, was finally shot down, falling onto the uncut Turkish wire.

Captain Harold Robert Clayton, 1/Lancashire Fusiliers, was killed on 4 June 1915, aged forty-one. He had previously served during the Boer War as a trooper in the East Kent Yeomanry, and with his return to England in 1901 he was commissioned into the Lancashire Fusiliers. His body was visible hanging from the Turkish wire at J.10 until two months later, when members of the King's Own Scottish Borderers recovered his remains for burial on 6 August 1915. His Commanding Officer wrote to his mother:

> *He certainly was loved by everyone, and was one of the best fellows I have ever met. Well, he died as he would have wished to die, leading the regiment he loved so well, and knowing what a glorious name it had already made for itself in Gallipoli. I wish he could have lived to know that we have been awarded three VCs[1] and I like to think that he would have been one of those chosen. I am sure no one can have deserved it better.*

Another officer wrote:

> *According to several wounded brother officers I met in Malta, he was the life and soul of the regiment during the time in Gallipoli. He was, I hear, always natural and cheerful, and had great influence in keeping up everyone's spirits. ...His loss will be felt dreadfully in the battalion where he was without doubt the most popular officer, and one who had a very great influence.*

After the war his grave could not be positively identified and today is commemorated on Special Memorial B. 8 in Twelve Tree Copse Cemetery. The epitaph on his gravestone reads: DEAR OLD HAROLD.

DEAR OLD HAROLD – Captain H. R. Clayton, 1/Lancashire Fusiliers, killed after reaching the Turkish wire at J.10. (© Chambers)

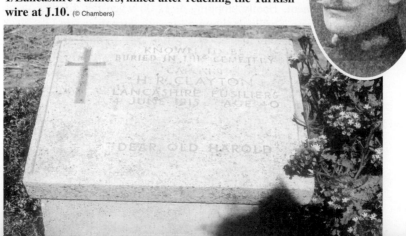

14/Sikhs at rest in Gully Ravine, June 1915. (Creighton)

The Sikhs had the advantage of some dead ground in the ravine where a little progress was made, but as soon as they emerged into the open, near J.10, the waiting Turks practically annihilated them with heavy, concentrated fire. A few Sikhs did reach the Turkish wire, but were very quickly mown down. Second-Lieutenant Reginald Savory, 14/Sikhs, who was wounded in the action, stated that:

> *Methods here seem to be based on a theory that all tactics are rot, and that the only way to do anything at all is to rush forward 'bald-headed', minus support, minus reserves, and in the end probably minus a limb or two. Hence causing the almost total wiping out of the 14th Sikhs on 4th June. We had as our own special task, to advance up a nullah (a thing which one has*

14/Sikhs in the trenches.

14/Sikhs at base in Gully Ravine, June 1915. (© Chambers)

always learned should never be done until all the ground commanding it is first seized) against the Turks who were in a wired trench at the end, and also on both sides and at the top, and their machine-guns took us in front and rear and from practically every side. (Needless to say we had no supports whatever! Not a damned thing!) Well at 12 noon, we got up out of our trenches, got through their barbed wire (the only regiment that did) and bagged their first trench: total time taken, roughly twenty minutes. We hung on there all right, unable to go forward because of having only two British officers left, and also because of their machine-guns..not a single reinforcement did we get after repeated messages had been sent, and at about 9 am next day we had to come back having had nine officers killed and three wounded out of fourteen, and the regiment being 135 strong...so bang goes one of the finest regiments of the Indian Army, and certainly the best on this old Peninsula.

The remaining Sikhs made a second attempt that day to advance up the ravine, but were cut down again by heavy Turkish fire as soon as they begun advancing along the gully floor. The concentration of fire almost wiped out the remnant of the battalion. That day it lost twelve British officers out of fifteen, eleven Indian Officers out of

We only got back the body of one of our British Officers. **Lieutenant Leonard Francis Cremen, aged twenty-six, 14/Sikhs, killed in the 4 June advance along Gully Ravine where the battalion lost eighty per cent of their officers. He is buried at Pink Farm Cemetery.**

fourteen and 380 men out of 514. Lieutenant Savory wrote:

Those damned Turks mutilated some our wounded, and fired on our stretcher-bearers and wounded, when they were trying to get back to cover. We only got back the body of one of our British Officers (Cremen). The others are still lying out there and so are all the rest of our dead.

Lieutenant Richard John Frederick Philip Meade, aged twenty-three, 14/Sikhs (King George's Own Ferozepore) was killed in action on 4 June. Meade went with his regiment to Egypt in November 1914, proceeding to Gallipoli in April 1915. Meade was wounded on 2 May, returning to duty a week later. His commanding officer wrote: *His death is a great loss to me and the regiment. He was killed on the 4 June, quite close to me. We were going towards my Adjutant, who was mortally wounded, when your son was shot through the head. He died instantaneously, and did not suffer at all. His body was recovered some days afterwards, and was buried by an Army Chaplain near the spot where he was killed. His body lies near that of Colonel Jacques, who was killed the same day...I had the greatest admiration for your son. He was a splendid officer, conscientious and thoroughly reliable. I looked upon him as a man who would go far and make a name for himself.* Meade was mentioned in despatches twice. He is buried at Pink Farm Cemetery.

There were other successes that day, with some Turkish positions being captured, but unfortunately owing to lack of support, the captured trenches had to be relinquished. Elements of 6/Gurkha, under Captain C. W. Birdwood, gained their objective by covertly approaching the Mushroom Redoubt, on the extreme left of J.11 trench, from beneath the cliffs. Before the Turks knew what was happening, the Gurkhas had captured the redoubt and the northwest part of J.11. Unfortunately, owing to lack of support and a sufficient number of bombs to counter

Indian AT Cart on the Beach Road.

the Turks' plentiful supply, the pinned in Gurkhas had to finally evacuate the position, covered by the naval guns of HMS *Wolverine*.

Captain C. W. Birdwood, 6/Gurkha Rifles, was mortally wounded on 4 June attack on Mushroom Redoubt for which he was recommended the DSO. He succumbed to his wounds on 7 June at the 108/Indian Field Ambulance at Gully Beach, aged thirty-three, and is buried in Pink Farm Cemetery. The war diary of the 108/Indian Field Ambulance on June 7 noted:

(© Chambers

> *Captain Birdwood, who appeared to be doing well all day yesterday, suddenly showed symptoms of acute peritonitis at 5 p.m., & at 8 p.m. his condition became very bad. He died at 12.40 a.m. at a very rapid course.*

Brigadier-General Cox wrote,

> *...not only is he a loss to the Brigade, but to the whole Army. His daring as a scout, and his spirit of offensive, were the success of the advance on the left.*

A second assault to retake the Mushroom Redoubt and J.11 was ordered, and this time the opportunity was given to the newly arrived 5/Gurkha, which had only disembarked the previous day. The plan was to attack the position by the same route that had proved successful earlier in the day, even though surprise was now obviously lost. The 1/Royal Dublin Fusiliers attempted an attack at the Gully Ravine end of J.11 in support the Gurkhas, but came under heavy fire where the Sikhs met their end earlier. The RDF never managed to reach J.11, the heavy fire forcing them to withdraw. By the cliffs, under a hail of shrapnel and rifle fire, the Gurkhas got as far as the dead ground below the redoubt, only to be showered with Turkish bombs, which were rolled down the hill and caused many casualties. The Gurkhas hung on

View from Gully Spur overlooking the field hospitals on the beach. 108/Indian Field Ambulance was located below. (IWM Q13339)

to this dangerous position until dusk, when they were eventually ordered to withdraw. Both assaults were predestined to failure; the element of surprise had gone, leaving the positions firmly in the Turkish hands.

Reverend Creighton's diary entry for 4 June:

> *The gully was in a perfect turmoil, of course, guns going off on all sides, and the crack of the bullets tremendously loud. They swept down the gully, and one or two men were hit. I cannot imagine anything much more blood-curdling than to go up the gully for the first time while a fierce battle is raging. You cannot see a gun anywhere, or know where the noise is coming from. At the head of the gully you simply go up the side right into the trenches. You see nothing except men passing to and fro at the bottom, and there is the incessant din overhead.*[2]

The attacks that day in the British centre and on the right began very successfully, with three lines of trenches almost a kilometre wide being captured. However most of this ground had to be evacuated owing to lack of support and the failure of neighbouring attacks. Second-Lieutenant George Raymond Dallas Moor of 2/Hampshires advanced with his battalion, capturing two lines of trenches on Fir Tree Spur, H.8-H.9 and also H.10. Casualties had been heavy, and Moor, only eighteen years old, was one of the few officers left. In the early morning of 6 June the Turks attacked and recaptured H.12, the most advanced trench 88 Brigade had taken the day before. The Turks reached the second line, but were driven back with heavy losses. The shock of the Turkish advance initially caused the British trench garrisons to fall back *en masse* to H.11 under a heavy fire. Troops in H.11, seeing the troops in front falling back, also began to flee, to be rallied at the last moment by Moor. His citation for the Victoria Cross reads:

> *For most conspicuous bravery and resource on the 5th June 1915 [sic], during operations south of Krithia, Dardanelles. When a detachment of a battalion on his left, which had lost all its officers, was rapidly retiring before a heavy Turkish attack,*

A contemporary artist's impression of Second-Lieutenant G. R. D. Moor winning his VC. Moor was the youngest army officer VC of the war.

Second Lieutenant Moor, immediately grasping the danger to the remainder of the line, dashed back some 200 yards, stemmed the retirement, led back the men and recaptured the lost trench. This young officer, who only joined the Army in October 1914, by his personal bravery and presence of mind, saved a dangerous situation.

H.11 was recaptured, but H.12 remained in Turkish hands. Moor, the youngest army officer VC of the war, was evacuated from Gallipoli with dysentery in September 1915. He later served on the Western Front, but died of influenza in November 1918, eight days before the armistice was signed. He is buried at Y Farm Military Cemetery, near Armentieres, France.

The attack's failure on Gully Spur was arguably due to the weakness of the artillery support. This failed to cut the Turkish wire and destroy their entrenched positions, and at the last moment it was diverted to support the attack on Fir Tree Spur. The heavy machine gun and rifle fire from the Turkish posts on both banks of Gully Ravine proved devastating to the advancing troops, whom the Turks were able to destroy with ease from behind the protection of their barbed wire.

Because the Lancashire Fusilier attack failed in the middle of the Indian Brigade, this neutralised the success of the Gurkhas nearer the coast, and of the 14/Sikhs in Gully Ravine. This failure on Gully Spur in turn affected the 88 Brigade's advance east of the ravine, which found its left flank wide open and enfiladed from across the ravine. It soon became clear to all that the whole attack was a failure. Reverend Creighton arrived on Gully Beach on 5 June, and describes in his diary:

The place was very full of wounded, who were being got off on boats as quickly as possible. Everywhere, of course, I was hearing about the battle. The left had been held up, unable to advance. The centre had advanced. The casualties were heavy. The whole situation was terrible – no advance, and nothing but casualties, and the worst was that the wounded had not been got back, but lay between ours and the Turks' firing line. It was impossible to get at some of them. The men said they could see them move. The firing went on without ceasing.

The Turks were in a critical position too, with an estimated 9,000 casualties, and their lines were barely holding together. The hope of a breakthrough, which had been so close, was past, as the British had fought themselves to a standstill, suffering about 4,500 casualties in the process. The Turks were by now well-recognised as a brave and determined opponent, a force to be reckoned with, in contrast to the pre-war perception that was based on their poor performance and subsequent defeat during the Balkans War of 1912/13.

Sergeant S. Evans, 1/Border Regiment, provides a detailed description of Gully Ravine conditions during this time.

We soon descend a rough pathway to the shore again where we are sheltered from the enemy's view and what is still better, from his shells as well. We then arrive at the entrance to a ravine, which winds its way through the centre of the Peninsula and from which we can reach our position under cover. This ravine is known locally as the Saghir Dere but has been nicknamed by the troops 'The Valley of Death' presumably on account of the number of small cemeteries that have been laid out in it. This is the main line of communication between the landing places and the line of the British trenches higher up the Peninsula.

The march up and down this ravine in marching order is trying in the extreme. It is covered with fine dry sand, which soon

The Gully Road – *Death was at work there, ...Death lived there, ...Death wandered up and down there and fed on Life.* (© Chambers)

covers us from head to foot. It penetrates one ear's, nose and mouth till one is nearly choked with it. There is little sign of any vegetation with the exception of some fine withered-looking and scorched grass and sand seems to be the order of the day. On the whole we appear to have landed at a very inhospitable spot.

A short march up the ravine and we reach the Headquarters of our Battalion which is at present in the trenches. However we do not go straight to the trenches but are halted whilst we have some breakfast of fried but fat bacon and hard biscuits washed down with a welcome draft of tea without milk.

The sun has now become very hot and we soon find another unwelcome enemy in our midst. The plague of flies is worse than one can imagine. They are present in millions and settle on one's food until it is almost in the mouth. A tin of tea will soon contain dozens of them struggling in the liquid whilst there is no part of the bare human body that they will not attack. Through the whole campaign the fly was one of our worst enemies. They would settle on the dead in clouds and the agony of the wounded was invariably added to by these pests settling on the bleeding wounds of the sufferer.

As we sit at our breakfast a constant stream of stretcher bearers is winding its way with the wounded to the numerous little dressing stations situated in little inlets of the main gully. Some are obviously badly hurt judging by their groans. Others not so badly hurt seem to be relieved at the idea of a little rest from the turmoil that they had to endure. Occasionally a

Bathers along the pier on Gully Beach – *if one was not too fastidious to object to coal-dust and refuse from lighters, nor to the close companionship of the dead horses and mules that floated around.* (CHAMBERS)

Ambulance wagon led by horses through the mud – *It was a bit rough going up, just enough room for one wagon but you got used to it.* (IWM Q13642)

stretcher will pass with the face of its human burden covered up. He has passed beyond all human aid and his destination will be one of the little cemeteries that we have already observed.

Rest was impossible. The flies see to that. In addition a battery of our guns just above the gully is engaged in blazing away at the enemy positions to the accompaniment of a series of ear splitting crashes so that although we are tired out from want of sleep, sleep is out of the question.

In reality the word 'rest' to the troops meant tiring fatigues all day and night, digging lots of new trenches, strengthening and lengthening existing ones and digging dugouts. Unloading the lighters at Gully Beach was a two-way process; carry a large rock down to the beach to reinforce the pier and then return with boxes of stores from the boats.

The beach fatigues however did sometimes offer a chance of a swim:

> ...if one was not too fastidious to object to coal-dust and refuse from lighters, nor to the close companionship of the dead horses and mules that floated around. These were constantly being towed out to sea, but the homing instinct, or the current, brought them back again.[5]

The trenches were very narrow, and when troops entered or left the lines there was often the chance they would meet another party going the other way. Trying to pass one another in these cramped conditions led to delay and confusion for many of the officers and men. Once in the line, be it the front, support or reserve trench, one could then sit on the fire step, equipment and rifle at the ready in case of any sudden call. Rifle fire during the day was mainly sporadic, but during the night it was often never-ending, as this was the time when No Man's Land came to life. The Turks especially feared night attacks and their rifles fired continually throughout the night, along with the occasional crash of a shell, short burst of machine-gun fire or the illumination of a Very light or a ship's searchlight. It was not uncommon for jumpy sentries to fire off a shot at a shadow in No Man's Land, and then ignite the whole line into a frenzy of small arms fire:

> Indeed a heavy fire was once opened on what proved to be an advance in open order by two large hedgehogs.[6]

Boomerang and the Turkey Trench

During the night of 10/11 June detachments from the 2/South Wales Borderers and 1/Border Regiment made a raid on two old Turkish trench systems (marked A and the line B to C) that jutted out from the eastern side of Gully Ravine. Both of these positions needed capturing

Map 10. The Boomerang and Turkey Trench, June 1915

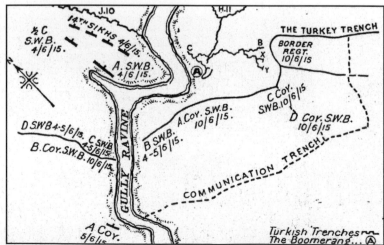

to straighten out the British line. The southern and short trench (A) was known as the Boomerang, because of its general shape, and the northern or longer piece was called Turkey Trench (B to C). Both of these had resisted capture by 88 Brigade during the 4 June attack.

Heavy and fierce fighting in the Boomerang saw the South Wales Borderers enter it and be repelled three times by determined Turkish bomb attacks from the direction of Gully Ravine. The Border Regiment then succeeded in capturing the whole of Turkey Trench, thus cutting off the Boomerang. However, they were soon compelled to evacuate most of this trench owing to a stubborn Turkish counter-attack that forced them out, leaving them with only about seventy yards of the trench, which they quickly reinforced with a barricade:

> *Rifle fire continued without intermission throughout the whole night. Shortly after midnight our guns from behind us join in and the din becomes terrific. The continuous crashing of the artillery, the momentary glare of the flashes, the pale ghostly illumination of the Very lights, added to the heavy rifle fire and the staccato rat tat of the machine guns, combine to create a vivid impression of hell let loose.*

The Turks were determined to eject the British from their part of Turkey Trench, and threw down a heavy bombardment in the early morning. This fell on Turkey Trench and the support lines:

The Boomerang site today. (© Chambers)

A contemporary drawing of the night attack on the Boomerang and Turkey Trench.

The distant boom of the guns, sounding somewhat like the beating of a distant drum, is followed by a strange whirring noise and almost immediately a series of shells burst with a terrific crash about 10 yards behind our trench, sending up a cloud of earth and black, evil smelling fumes. First the front trenches receive about ten minutes of treatment, then they range again on to our line till one does not know where to expect them next. As one hears the peculiar 'whirr' one involuntarily crouches as far as possible into the trench, expecting every minute that the next one will land in our midst. Then – the crash as the shell lands just behind or just in front and we are lucky to escape with a shower of earth on us.

As this continues one's nerves become more and more highly strung until we heartily pray for them to finish. One young lad in my platoon soon gave way under it and was grovelling hysterically on the ground. This makes the rest even worst and for the sake of the 'morale' of the rest he is eventually sent down to the gully below.

Lieutenant Rupert Charles Inglis, 2/South Wales Borderers, led one of the raids on the Boomerang, and his brother, **Lieutenant H. J. Inglis**, led a second raid. Both Inglis brothers showed the greatest gallantry and determination in these attacks, both being wounded as a result, and both being recommended for the Military Cross. Only H. J. Inglis received it. Rupert was wounded again on 28 June, dying of his wounds aboard a hospital ship the following day, where he was then buried at sea, aged thirty-one years. He is commemorated on the Helles Memorial.

Captain Reginald Henry Hamilton Moore, 1/Border Regiment, aged thirty, was killed on 11 June. On that day the Turks had succeeded in occupying part of the trench held by Captain Moore's company and were now attacking the Borders with bombs, making the position extremely difficult to retain. Captain Moore rushed down the trench, followed by his men, and succeeded in clearing part of the trench practically unaided, but was shot dead while giving directions about strengthening the position. Captain Moore, mentioned in despatches for the action, was originally buried in Gully Cemetery, and today is buried in Twelve Tree Copse Cemetery.

The Turks tried several times to recapture the rest of Turkey Trench, culminating in another fierce bomb attack during the night of 15/16 June. This attack was supported by a heavy Turkish artillery bombardment on the British lines, that paved the way for their attack. The Dublin Fusiliers, who were holding the trench at the time, were forced to retire under this hailstorm of fire, losing the trench to the Turks. At 05:00 however the Munster Fusiliers made a surprise bombing counter-attack that recaptured all this lost ground.

Sergeant Dennis Moriarty, 1/Royal Munster Fusiliers, wrote in his diary:

> *An officer, a sergeant and a couple of men sapped up to within about 20 yards of the trench which the Turks were in and started to sling bombs into it for all they were worth. It was a complete surprise to the Turks who did not expect this movement but there was still another shock waiting them. While the bomb throwers were getting ready two of our machine guns took up a position where they would be able to get anyone leaving the trench. Consequently when the bombs started to drop in the trench the Turks took to their heels but every one of them were brought down by our machine guns at point blank range. The machine gun officer estimated that there were at least 400 of them there so that was a little bit of our debt paid off.*

Whilst Turkey Trench was back in British hands, the Boomerang remained firmly held by the Turks, and they quickly set about strengthening the position, turning it into a formidable redoubt.

At 18:30, on 18 June, whilst Sir Ian Hamilton and his staff were having a special dinner on Imbros to commemorate the 100th Anniversary of the Battle of Waterloo, the Turks commenced a tremendous bombardment of the British trenches east of Gully Ravine. It was later estimated that around 500 high explosive shells fell in the space of thirty minutes. A follow-up Turkish infantry attack, centring mainly on Turkey Trench, began at about 20:30. The initial attack was successfully driven off, but a second attack succeeded in forcing the 2/South Wales Borderers out of their trench, leaving a gap in the British line. The neighbouring 1/Royal Inniskilling Fusiliers immediately came under a Turkish bomb attack that forced them to relinquish a further thirty yards of trench. Captain Gerald Robert O'Sullivan, with a party of Inniskillings, armed with a meagre supply of jam-tin bombs, regained the lost thirty yards of trench and began to bomb their way along the rest of the trench towards the Turks. The rest of the battle raged backwards and forwards, but O'Sullivan held on in his desperately recaptured position.

The SWB managed to launch a counter-attack at 03:30 to try to relieve the pressure on O'Sullivan, but the Turks repulsed this successfully. At 04:30 Brigadier-General W. R. Marshall (GOC, 87 Brigade) ordered a joint assault by both the SWB and Inniskillings. O'Sullivan led the way. The Inniskillings' War Diary states:

Captain G. R. O'Sullivan, 1/Royal Inniskilling Fusiliers. His bombing action at Turkey Trench, on 18 June, contributed to his later award of the VC.

4.30 a.m. Capt O'Sullivan with bomb party of about 6 men together with SWB bomb party drove enemy down Turkish sap. Enemy then endeavoured to evacuate sap by retiring across the open, but were shot down by rapid fire from A and B Coys. Remainder of enemy in Turkish Sap (13) taken prisoners.

It was not all over yet. By 05:15 about thirty yards of the trench had been recaptured by the British, but it was not until 10:00 that the head of Turkey Trench was eventually reached. In this action O'Sullivan *behaved magnificently throughout*, and a later action on the night of 1 July, 1915, ensured an award of the Victoria Cross.

Casualties to both sides were very heavy. Nearly a hundred dead Turks were reported in or within ten yards of Turkey Trench. This was only a small proportion of their casualties, as many more lay further out. They were not alone, as the SWB and Inniskillings also suffered heavily. Later on, during 19 June, the Turks commenced a fresh bombardment, and tried to bring more reinforcements from the Gully and the Boomerang in preparation for another assault. It was reported that the Turks left their trenches very half-heartedly, and met a wall of lead as the SWB poured fire into them. This daylight attack soon petered out. For now, at least, this front quietened down a little.

1. Actually six VCs were awarded to the 1/Lancashire Fusiliers for the W Beach Landings, although at this time only three awards had been announced. These were to Captain R. R. Willis, Sergeant A. Richards and Private W. Keneally. It was not until 1917 that Captain C. Bromley, Corporal J. Grimshaw and Sergeant F. Stubbs were given the award.
2. Creighton, Reverend Oswin, CF, *With the Twenty Ninth Division in Gallipoli: A Chaplain's Experience*, (1916), p.121.
3. Ibid., pp.122-123.
4. My Gallipoli Story by Sgt. S. Evans, *The Gallipolian*, Spring and Autumn 1984 editions.
5. Gibbon, Frederick P., *The 42nd (East Lancashire) Division 1914-1918*,(1920), p.50.
6. Atkinson, C. T, *The History of the South Wales Borderers 1914-1918*, (1931), p.114.
7. My Gallipoli Story by Sgt. S. Evans, *The Gallipolian*, Autumn 1984, No.45, pp.23-24.
8. Atkinson, *Op.Cit.*, (1931), p.121.

Chapter Three

THE PLAN OF ATTACK

Sir Ian Hamilton was anxious to strike while the iron was hot and build on the recent successes of General Gouraud's French attack on 21 June. In this attack the French had managed to push the Allied right forward, capturing a number of trenches on the big spur west of the Kerevez Dere. Both the heavily defended Turkish redoubts called 'Haricot' and 'Quadrilateral' fell to the French during this battle. The latter, which witnessed a lot of heavy fighting, was only completely captured on 30 June. Hamilton wanted to exploit the advantage as soon as possible, but had to delay the attack until the morning of the 28 June[1] to allow adequate time for preparation.

The success of the French attack had been largely due to their artillery support, an important point that Hamilton and his staff noted. Several of the earlier attacks failed owing to lack of artillery, and without adequate artillery support it was doubtful that this one would succeed. To supplement the low numbers of British high explosive shells, it was necessary to borrow two trench howitzers from the French for the attack. These were brought into position for 28 June.

Because the Turkish flank on Gully Spur was exposed to enfilade fire from British warships, and thus regarded by them as a point of great danger, the defences they had built here consisted of five lines of

A 4.5″ howitzer from 460/Battery, above Y Beach, June 1915.

460/Howitzer Battery Observation Post, June 1915. (© Chambers)

narrow but deep trenches. This represented a formidable defensive position, which also contained tactically positioned and strengthened machine-gun redoubts. If the artillery did not destroy these, they would seriously hamper the British attack. The five lines of Turkish trenches were named J.9, J.10, J.11, J.12 and J.13, all positioned on Gully Spur, linked together by a long transverse trench called J.11a, which crowned the face of the cliff. The two furthest trenches, J.12 and J.13, formed the right flanks of an immediate trench system with H.12, H.12a and H.14 beyond, positioned on Fir Tree Spur. The Turks had only begun working on these new lines recently, and had been almost wholly unmolested by the British artillery. This was due to the British shortage of ammunition and the strict injunction that not more than two rounds per gun per day were to be expended except in the case of an attack. The new trench lines, however, was still uncompleted, and consisted mainly of short lines of unconnected trenches that contained no deep dugouts and were only fronted by a minimal amount of wire. The Turkish wire was a lot heavier and thicker than the British wire, which caused problems with the standard issue British wire-cutters, which proved virtually useless in many cases. However, the wire's weight on top of simple wooden trestles often caused it to lie too close

Lancashire Street's 18pdr in action: the most advanced gun on the Peninsula. (IWM Q14839)

RFA signallers in a trench. *'Telephone wires were laid everywhere in the trenches, and telephone operators and observing officers were scattered up and down the line. On the first sign of an enemy attack these officers communicated with their Batteries in the rear, and within two seconds a curtain of fire was rained on the advancing foe'* (LIEUTENANT-COLONEL J. H. PATTERSON). (© Chambers)

to the ground, enabling it to be fairly easily trampled over.

Bearing in mind the lessons learned from the Third Battle of Krithia, Hunter-Weston decided to attack on both sides of Gully Ravine at the same time, up to the mouth of the tributary called the Nullah. The plan was to capture trenches J.12 and J.13 on Gully Spur, and H.12 and H.12a on Fir Tree Spur. This advance, on a frontage of nearly 700 yards, would outflank the Turkish position in the centre,

placing the British on the seaward flank of Krithia, thus securing a valuable foothold in this sector. The opportunity needed to be seized while these trenches lay in an unfinished state. This would not be easy, as the Turkish positions in the area were undeniably strong, consisting of several redoubts heavily armed with Maxim machine guns and capable of all-round defence. There was a sizeable amount of barbed wire in front of the Turkish trenches, but not the huge amounts seen on the

Western Front. Wire was not reaching the Turks in large enough quantities to provide a serious obstacle. Although the Turks had as yet constructed no deep dugouts in the area, their end of Gully Ravine did provide deep and numerous tributaries that offered excellent cover to their troops, stores and their reserves. The 11th Turkish Division manned this line, whilst the 6th Turkish Division was in reserve, behind Hill 472. Turkish artillery in the area consisted of approximately ten field and mountain batteries and a further ten medium to heavy howitzers.

Hunter-Weston placed Major-General Beauvoir de Lisle, GOC 29th Division, in command of the attack, leaving all the infantry planning to him. The 29th Division was much weakened, having been in the field continuously since the landings. To supplement numbers, 29 Indian Brigade, and the newly arrived 156 Brigade[2] from Major-General Granville Egerton's 52nd (Lowland) Division, were attached for the attack. 86, 87 and 29 Indian Brigades were to attack the J trenches along Gully Spur, including Gully Ravine, whilst 156 Brigade and 88 Brigade were to be used to attack the H trenches on Fir Tree Spur. A diversionary attack was also to be made at Anzac, on the same day, in the hope of diverting reinforcements, which might otherwise be available to help the Turks opposing the main attack in the south.

The artillery was under the direct command of Brigadier-General Sir Hugh Simpson Baikie, although de Lisle was free to express his wishes as to the distribution of the guns available. The Allied artillery consisted of seventy-seven guns, including twelve British and nine French howitzers, and also the further support of the navy with a cruiser, HMS *Talbot*, and two destroyers, HMS *Scorpion* and HMS *Wolverine*, all lying off the western coast. British ammunition reserves were meagre, with very few high explosive rounds available. Nevertheless, by sanctioning the use of nearly a third of the total stock of ammunition at Helles for this one small operation, it was possible to allot a larger proportion of shells to the frontage of attack than in any previous British action on Gallipoli. Actual expenditure greatly exceeded the 12,000 rounds of allotted ammunition totalling over 16,000 rounds; this total also excluded those expended by the navy, for which no records now appear to be available. During the Third Battle of Krithia, on 4 June, only 11,000 rounds were used, and these were expended over a far greater area. Earlier still, during the Second Battle of Krithia, on 6 May, 20,000 troops were supported over three days by an average of 6,000 rounds a day. In France, at the Battle of Aubers Ridge on 9 May 1915, 80,000 rounds were fired in the course of a

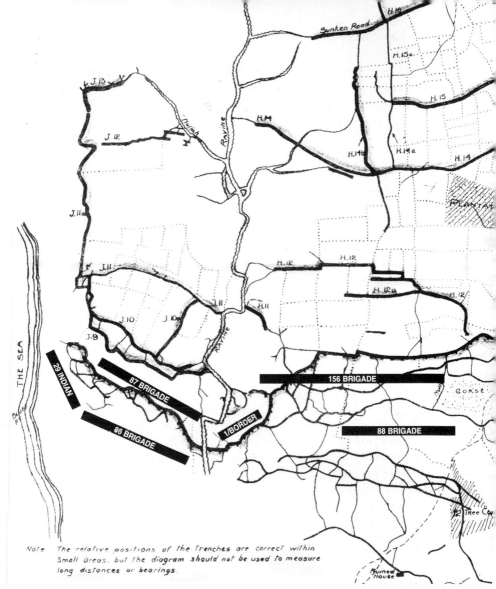

Map 11. Trench map showing Brigade positions for 28 June 1915.

single day supported 30,000 troops. Unfortunately, at this stage one of the problems facing Hamilton was not only lack of shell but also the War Office. No one had calculated the amount of ammunition for a prolonged occupation of the Gallipoli Peninsula. Additionally the supply organisation at this stage of the campaign was very bad. One transport ship, for example, arrived at Helles with a cargo of much needed shells, but without the necessary fuses. When the fuses eventually did arrive on a further transport, there were no tools

One of 460 Battery's 4.5″ Howitzers, concealed at Y Ravine in June 1915.
(© Chambers)

included. It took a third ship to bring the necessary fuse tools. Hamilton was in dire need of shells and troops, but requests at this time were just answered by London with 'push on'. The drain on stores and resources of a major campaign on two fronts had become a critical issue for the War Office. Taking supplies from one front to aid the other was not a solution. If the manpower and artillery support used during the failed attack at Aubers Ridge on the Western Front were made at Gallipoli, Hamilton would have had an excellent chance of 'pushing on'. This arguably could have led to victory on the Peninsula, an opened Dardanelles, and the fleet at its goal of Constantinople.

The 29th Division's instructions for 156 Brigade were:

> *The task of capturing the H12 line has on previous occasions proved easy. Failure to retain possession has been due to want of support on the left of the line* [i.e. Gully Spur]*, which will now be forthcoming... It is anticipated that the artillery bombardment on this occasion, which is more intense than any in Flanders in support of our troops, will render the task of the brigade easy.*

This statement may have had some effect in giving the troops an added degree of confidence and encouragement, but it soon became clear that the artillery support for their attack on the H trenches along Fir Tree Spur was to be a lot less concentrated than that given to the J trench assault along Gully Spur. The reason for this was that the task of

An 18-pdr field gun at Helles. (© Chambers)

The 'iron harvest' in the Turkish War Relics Museum at Morto Bay.
(© Chambers)

capturing Gully Spur, with its five lines of trenches, was thought to be the most difficult and also the most important part of the attack. Unfortunately no more guns were available to give 156 Brigade any further artillery support, and the support that they did have consisted only of four and a half batteries of 18-pdrs with no high explosive, just a limited supply of shrapnel. Shrapnel was good for dealing with infantry in the open, but arguably less effective in destroying wire entanglements and entrenched positions. High explosives was the answer at the time. General Simpson Baikie commented on the artillery support for 156 Brigade:

> *Before the action the Corps Commander sent for me to say that he did not consider that enough guns and ammunition had been allotted to this portion of the Turkish trenches. I replied that I agreed, but that there were no more available, and that to reduce the bombardment of the hostile trenches on the left of our front would gravely prejudice the success of the 29th Division in that quarter, and that I understood success there was more vital than on our right flank. After consultation with the G.O.C. 29th Division, the Corps Commander agreed with my allotment of the artillery. We then did our utmost to obtain the loan of more guns, howitzers or ammunition from the French without success and with the result that the attack was beaten off.*

Hamilton later remarked in his diary that, 'Baikie is crying out to us for shells as if we were bottling them up! There are none'.[3] The plan was that 87 Brigade was thus to take five lines of trenches with overwhelming artillery support, whilst 156 Brigade was to take two lines with practically none at all. The results were predictable.

De Lisle planned the operation very thoroughly (see Appendix I), aware that many of his officers had only recently arrived and were fairly inexperienced. The 2/South Wales Borderers, for example, had a rehearsal of the operation the day before the attack, so that every NCO

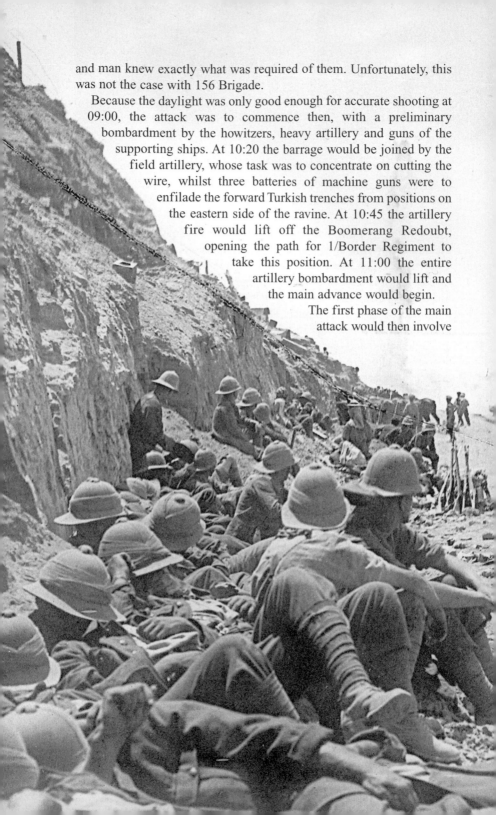

and man knew exactly what was required of them. Unfortunately, this was not the case with 156 Brigade.

Because the daylight was only good enough for accurate shooting at 09:00, the attack was to commence then, with a preliminary bombardment by the howitzers, heavy artillery and guns of the supporting ships. At 10:20 the barrage would be joined by the field artillery, whose task was to concentrate on cutting the wire, whilst three batteries of machine guns were to enfilade the forward Turkish trenches from positions on the eastern side of the ravine. At 10:45 the artillery fire would lift off the Boomerang Redoubt, opening the path for 1/Border Regiment to take this position. At 11:00 the entire artillery bombardment would lift and the main advance would begin.

The first phase of the main attack would then involve

87 Brigade taking the first three trenches on Gully Spur, J.9, J.10 and J.11 including Gully Ravine up to this point. On the eastern flank the newly arrived 156 Brigade (52nd Division) was to capture the whole of Fir Tree Spur. Units of 29 Indian Brigade were to occupy trench J.11a when captured and also advance along the cliff to provide support to the left flank of 87 Brigade.

The second phase would commence at 11:30, which would have 86 Brigade leapfrogging 87 Brigade, in order to capture trenches J.12 and J.13. They would then dig a new line from J.13 across to the Nullah, and then by extending it over to the eastern bank of the ravine, meet up with trench H.12. The Indian Brigade would continue support along the cliff tops, consolidating the length of trench J.11a and extending this line down to the shore.

All infantry battalions were to attack in three lines, consisting of the assaulting wave, support and reserve. The leading waves were ordered to attack with the bayonet in a quick rush, not to stop and fire; speed was of the essence. In addition to their fighting kit, every man was to

Troops resting on the beach road, near Gully Ravine, June 1915. (IWM Q13342)

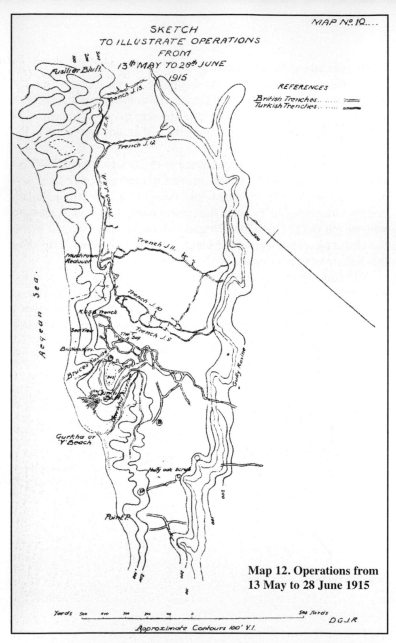

SKETCH
TO ILLUSTRATE OPERATIONS
FROM
13th MAY TO 28th JUNE
1915

MAP No. 12....

REFERENCES
British Trenches........
Turkish Trenches........

Fusilier Bluff.

Trench J.13.

Trench J.12.

Trench J.11.

Mushroom Redoubt

Trench J.10.

K.O.S.B. Trench

Trench J.9.

Sea View

The Nip

Bruces Ravine

Gurkha or 'Y' Beach

Gully Ravine

Holly oak scrub

Point P.

Aegean Sea.

**Map 12. Operations from
13 May to 28 June 1915**

Yards 500   400   300   200   100   0   500 Yards

D.G.J.R.

Approximate Contours 100' V.I.

carry two empty sandbags, to be tucked into their webbing waist belts, to be used in repairing and reversing the parapets of the captured trenches and also to help in barricading enemy communication trenches. Owing to the great heat, their heavy packs were not to be carried, but stacked out of the way. At this stage of the campaign the

74

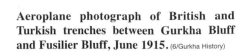

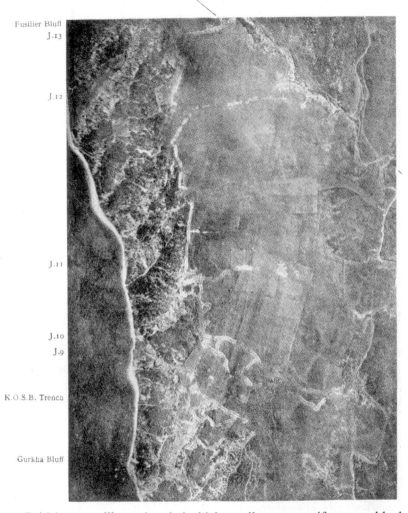

British were still wearing their thick woollen serge uniforms, and had only been recently issued with sun 'pith' helmets. Owing to the enormous officer casualties, all officers were instructed to wear the serge 'tommies' tunics, referred to as 'funk' or 'wind-up' jackets, in order to blend in with the other ranks. To assist the artillery every third man was to attach to his back a large piece of tin made from either biscuit or kerosene tins, an idea developed by Brigadier-General

William Marshall. The 29th Division had an equilateral triangular piece with one-foot sides, and 156 Brigade a rectangular piece. These were to be connected by two loops of string to the shoulders, designed to flash in the sun to identify their positions. It was intended that these shining pieces of tin be placed on the back (parados) of the captured trench to show the furthest points penetrated. Each battalion was additionally to carry two red/khaki canvas screens each, to be erected by day in the rear of a trench in order to request additional artillery support if required. The screens were previously used on the 4 June Krithia attack (red with a white diagonal line, to face the British lines, khaki the enemy's line), but largely failed due to the Turks counter-attacking the trenches and the screens being lost in these attacks, or the men carrying them killed. By night Very flare pistols would be used, although the field telephone was the preferred method of communication, as long as the lines were not cut.

Another complication at this stage of the campaign was the mismatch of rifle and ammunition. The newly arrived 156 Brigade were issued with the older Long Lee-Enfield rifle as used in the Boer War, instead of the newer Short Magazine Lee-Enfield (SMLE) that the 29th Division was using. Some of the older models had their breeches strengthened to fire the newer Mark VII .303 round, as used in the SMLE. Others did not, and these, if mistakenly fired with a Mark VII round, would behave very erratically and eventually the rifle would be ruined. The Long Lee was also issued at this time to other units at Gallipoli, including the 42nd Division, Indian Brigade and the Royal Naval Division. Later in the campaign the SMLE became the standard issue rifle. The same problem existed with ammunition for the older Maxim gun (Mark VI .303 round) and the newer Vickers (Mark VII .303 round). These problems further complicated the administration of ammunition supply to the front line units, especially when they were mixed, until the SMLE and Vickers became the standard issue weapons.

87 Brigade's orders were to assault the Boomerang, and trenches J.9,

Panoramic view of Gully Spur from the sea. (© Chambers)

FUSILIER BLUFF ECHELONS BORDER RAVINE ESSEX RAVINE

TROLLEY RAVINE

J.10, J.11, including the gully up to this point, and half of J.11a. The 1/Border Regiment was to make the assault on the Boomerang. The Borders were to move up the ravine in order to rush the Boomerang redoubt and the small portion of Turkey Trench still held by the Turks. This was the most advanced part of the Turkish line, heavily fortified with a triple depth of wire, behind which lay the machine guns, holding this vital strategic point from which Turkish fire could sweep all the surrounding area, especially that on Gully Spur. Because of this all previous advances in the area had been unable to avoid huge casualties. Three attempts had already been made to capture this redoubt, all failing. A lot of emphasis was now placed on its capture, which was planned for fifteen minutes before the main assault. Unless this could be achieved immediately, the whole advanced would be delayed, possibly causing the whole operation in this sector to fail.

When this position was captured, the Borders then had to clear Gully Ravine as far north as its junction with J.11. The 2/South Wales Borderers were to capture J.9 and J.10 and the 1/Inniskilling and 1/KOSB were to leapfrog them and capture J.11 and the southern half of J.11a.

29 Indian Brigade's task was to advance along the cliffs between the crest and the sea, and then take over J.11a and J.11, which should have been captured already by 87 Brigade. The 10/Gurkhas were to take part in the first stage and 6/Gurkha in the second. The 5/Gurkhas were in support. The 14/Sikhs were to hold the old British front line on Gully Spur after 86 Brigade advance.

86 Brigade's advance was planned to begin at 11:30, half an hour after the first infantry assault. Under the cover of artillery, advancing across the open from the cover of Bruce's Ravine, the 1/Royal Munster Fusiliers were to take the J.12 and J.13 trenches, whilst the Indian Brigade continued its advance up J.11a, protecting 86 Brigade's left flank. The 1/Lancashire Fusiliers were to act as the connecting link between the 2/Royal Fusiliers and 156 Brigade at H.12, advancing from Gurkha Ravine. The 1/Royal Dublin Fusiliers were to remain in Brigade reserve at Geoghegan's Bluff.

Three battalions (2/Hampshire Regiment, 1/Essex Regiment and

BRUCES RAVINE   GURKHA BLUFF   Y RAVINE   GURKHA RAVINE
Y OR GURKHA BEACH

View of the open ground on Fir Tree Spur where 156 Brigade would advance. The Turkish H.12 trenches were towards the middle of this field.
(© Chambers)

5/Royal Scots) of 88 Brigade were to be held in close support as Divisional reserve. Its fourth battalion (4/Worcestershire Regiment) was holding the old British front line between 156 Brigade and the left of the 42nd Division.

Sergeant S. Evans 1/Border Regiment recalls going into the line in the afternoon of Sunday, 27 June:

> *At 4.30 PM we dress in full marching order and set off up the Gully once again. The day is intensely hot, the hottest we have experienced so far and before we have gone far the perspiration is running off us like water. The heat and dust, together with the heavy weight of our equipment is trying to the most seasoned veterans and we are glad when we get a halt half way up.*[4]

Before they went into the trenches their chaplain conducted a brief service, which,

> *...brings home keenly to all the possibilities that the morrow holds and no church congregation could have been more reverent in its manner than this collection of rough manhood that made up our little Army. At the conclusion, led by the chaplain, the whole Brigade broke into that fine old Hymn 'Abide with Me' and at the concluding lines, 'In life, in death, O Lord abide with me', one felt that never before had any of us sung it with such real earnestness.*

The sunset that night was reported to have turned the sky into a deep blood red colour, an omen on this eve of battle.

156 Brigade was to assault H.12a, H.12, H.11 and the Nullah northeast of H.11 as far as the communication trench joining H.12 at the bend of the Nullah. These trenches followed the general line of the ridge that dominated this sector overlooking Gully Ravine. The frontage here was almost half a mile, and they had to be taken with basically no artillery support, something the Brigade did not realise, believing that the bombardment would be of equivalent force to that on Gully Spur.

The Brigade consisted of the 4/Royal Scots (Queen's Edinburgh

Rifles) on the left, 7/Royal Scots (Leith Rifles), which consisted of only two companies following the Gretna disaster, one of which was a company from the 8/Highland Light Infantry, were in the centre, with the 8/Cameronians (Scottish Rifles) on the right. The 7/Cameronians (Scottish Rifles) were held in Brigade reserve.

Gretna/Quintinshill Railway Disaster – 22 May 1915

The 7/Royal Scots left Larbert, Stirlingshire in two trains on Saturday 22 May 1915 for Liverpool. Lieutenant-Colonel Peebles with his HQ staff and 'A' and 'D' Companies (15 officers, 483 other ranks) occupied the first train, leaving Larbert at 03:45. At 06:45, just north of Gretna by the Quintinshill signal cabin, this troop train ploughed into some empty carriages of a local train that was left on the main railway line by mistake. The train collided at full speed, with enough force to cause many of the carriages to topple over. Seconds later, travelling north, an express train, running late and at high speed, ploughed into the wreckage of both trains that were blocking the line, immediately setting them on fire. The rolling stock of the troop train was made from wood, with gas oil lamps, these factors being the cause of the fire that swept quickly through the carriages.

Casualties were three officers, twenty-nine NCOs, and one hundred and eighty-two men killed, many burned to death. A further five officers and 219 other ranks were left injured, or suffering from shock. This was a crippling blow to the 7/Battalion, only seven officers and fifty-seven other ranks surviving the disaster. These were sent home the following day. Lieutenant-Colonel Peebles was left with only half a battalion ('B' and 'C' Companies) with which to sail to Gallipoli. Edinburgh wept at this loss; this loss was to worsen at the Battle of Gully Ravine, just one month later. After the accident the majority of the Royal Scots dead were buried in the Rosebank Cemetery in Leith. On 16 May 1916 a memorial to the 214 officers and men of the 7/Royal Scots was dedicated in the Rosebank Cemetery. A further memorial plaque appears on the platform at Larbert, the platform from which the 7/Royal Scots departed on that morning, and there is also a memorial at Gretna Green. Today this remains as the worst rail tragedy recorded in Britain.

In another incident two companies (A and B) of the 4/Royal Scots narrowly avoided disaster before they arrived on the Peninsula. On 12 June their naval transport, HMS *Reindeer*, collided in the dark with a hospital steamer called the SS *Immingham*. Luckily the *Immingham* was returning empty from the Peninsula. It quickly sank to the bottom. The damaged HMS *Reindeer* was forced to limp back to Mudros with its precious cargo of men. Hamilton praised the Battalion for its 'gallant behaviour...who upheld the highest traditions of the service' by not showing panic during this critical situation, all standing to attention in the Birkenhead drill. The 4/Royal Scots thus had a high reputation even before they landed on the Peninsula.[5]

bombs were still very scarce.

The famous Mills bomb, otherwise known as the No.5 Hand Grenade, saw only limited use at Gallipoli in comparison with the Jam Tin and Cricket Ball bombs, which was entirely due to lack a of adequate supplies. This was not just at Gallipoli, although here the British fared the worst, but also on the Western Front. The Mills bomb, although initially seeing service during the autumn and winter of 1915, never reached the front in large quantities until the following year, ready for the Somme offensive.

Monday, 28 June turned out to be another sweltering hot day, as the sun rose to its peak through the quivering air. There was scarcely a breath of wind about, typical of Gallipoli during this time of year. The flowers that adorned the Helles fields in April were now just withered stalks; the fierce summer and recent battles scorched the whole area.

Grant wrote of the lead up to the attack:

about 8 o'clock we had some breakfast and then had a final look round to see that all was ready and that every man knew his instructions. At 9 a.m. our bombardment commenced. At first we were rather surprised that the volume of artillery was not greater, later we were surprised that the volume of fire was so great!

The men were lying about in the trench, smoking and reading or laughing and chatting. They were in great spirits, but as time wore on and the din became greater, the strain became greater also. Occasionally a man would be led past with his nerves shattered, his hands manacled – a raving maniac for the time being. The shells, both Turkish and British, seemed to be bursting all round and over us, but we had not many casualties. The sun soon became obscured by the dust and smoke and the acrid smell of smoke became almost unbearable.

1. Incidentally this was an important date as exactly one year before, on 28 June 1914, the Austrian Archduke Franz Ferdinand was assassinated in Sarajevo, the spark that ignited the world into the Great War.
2. Landed at Helles on 13/14 June, and consisted of 4/Royal Scots (Queens Edinburgh Rifles), 7/Royal Scots (Leith Rifles), 7/Cameronians (Scottish Rifles), 8/Cameronians (Scottish Rifles)
3. Hamilton, Sir Ian, *Gallipoli Diary*, (1920), Vol.II, p.13.
4. 'My Gallipoli Story' by Sgt. S. Evans, *The Gallipolian*, No.45, Autumn 1984, p.28.
5. This was immediately likened to the *Birkenhead* when British troops, reinforcements for the Eighth Frontier War, had gone down with the iron paddle steamer, whilst standing to attention, off the African coast in 1852. The axiom 'women and children first' became the accepted procedure after this event. The 'Birkenhead Drill' was later immortalised by Rudyard Kipling in the verse 'Soldier an' Sailor Too'.
6. *Diary kept by the Officers of 'C' Company, 4th Battalion The Royal Scots (Queen's Edinburgh Rifles) during their journey to and stay on the Gallipoli Peninsula May and June 1915.* This was written by Captain R.W.G. Rutherford, killed 28 June, and 2/Lt. L.R.Grant.
7. The three are Captain Robert Sebag-Montefiore (buried in the Chatby Jewish Cemetery, Egypt), Second-Lieutenant Samuel Williams (buried at Lancashire Landing Cemetery) and Second-Lieutenant Frank Tuff (buried in the Pieta Military Cemetery in Malta). Captain H. H. Dawes, who was also wounded, survived the accident.
8. Dismounted for service at Gallipoli, they consisted of 1/East Kent Yeomanry, 1/West Kent Yeomanry and 1/Sussex Yeomanry.

Chapter Four

THE BATTLE OF GULLY RAVINE

At 09:00 the British bombardment began to pulverize the Turks, continuing until zero hour with ever increasing intensity. In reply to this the Turkish artillery countered, bombarding the British trenches, which were now filled and congested with three waves of men awaiting the attack. This kept the stretcher-bearers busy, and those who could be, were evacuated. The Turkish counter-bombardment continued, causing sufficiently heavy losses to 156 Brigade that it had to bring up a platoon of the 7/Cameronians from support just before zero hour in order to fill a gap in the line.

Major James Norman Henderson, aged thirty-four, 4/Royal Scots, was killed just prior to the assault on 28 June 1915. Major Henderson had both legs smashed during the Turkish counter bombardment, and whilst he was being attended to in a dugout in a support trench, another shell burst, killing him and all inside. His remains were recovered for burial; however, after the war his grave could not be positively identified, and he is thus commemorated on Special Memorial C. 330 in Twelve Tree Copse Cemetery.

The Boomerang Redoubt bombardment began, with the first bombs from the French mortars falling on the strongpoint with deadly accuracy. Petty Officer F. W. Johnston, a machine gunner, in the Royal Naval Armoured Car Division, RNAS[1] recalls that the bombs':

...flight was easy to follow & was wonderfully fascinating. Reaching a height of, perhaps, two hundred feet and appearing to be directly overhead, it slowly turned over & still more slowly (it seemed) began to descend. It almost imperceptibly drew away from us and landed with a dull thud on the outer works of the Boomerang. A remarkable silence followed & then tons of earth, sections of entanglements, bodies, clothes and limbs were sent into the sky. A terrific explosion of unparalleled violence, causing the earth upon which we stood to tremble & spreading its pungent fumes, like a mist over everything & everyone, was the result. Its terrifying roar re-echoed along the ravine until drowned by the ships' guns at sea. Before the air was clear another torpedo was fired.

83

At 10.40 the order went along the 1/Border Regiments trench line to fix bayonets as the artillery barrage reached its crescendo:

One further minute and the word 'Ready' is passed along. In that one minute we unconsciously take one look at the sun and the sea and involuntarily commend our bodies and souls to our Maker – and then before we realise it a hoarse shout of 'Over' and we are up the ladders and racing like the wind for the redoubt about 200 yards distant.[2]

The bombardment lifted off the Boomerang Redoubt at precisely 10:45, opening the way for the Borders to attack:

At quarter to eleven we heard a faint cheer and knew it must be the Border Regiment on our left storming the 'Boomerang' Redoubt. We peered excitedly over the parapet and could dimly distinguish through the smoke figures running across the open,[3]

wrote Second Lieutenant L. R. Grant. Three open lines emerged from their trenches, bayonets fixed, advancing through the lingering dust cloud of the bombardment. The heavily fortified Boomerang redoubt (sometimes called Boomerang Fort), along with almost a hundred dazed Turkish prisoners was quickly captured. Little return fire was given by the surprised defenders, and casualties were light. 'B' Company attacked the redoubt whilst 'A' Company attacked the neighbouring trench known as Turkey Trench[4]. The remaining companies of the Borders were in support. The attack on Turkey Trench, however, caused the Borders a lot more trouble than the redoubt. About forty yards of the trench, towards the rear of the enemy's barricade, was found filled in. This left the assaulting party in the open, and exposed to a murderous fire, mainly from a previously unlocated trench that ran from Turkey Trench to H.12. All ranks in the first wave assault were killed or wounded in crossing this ground. The support fared a little better, but suffered very heavily again from the hail of rifle fire and shrapnel. The few who managed to get across this ground successfully captured the enemy trench using 'bomb, bayonet and rifle butt', according to their regimental history.

Sub-Lieutenant Frank Yeo, 4/Squadron Royal Naval Armoured Car Division, RNAS, who commanded a machine gun supporting the attack wrote:

The prisoners are fine looking men. Our Tommies are extraordinary, they are now giving them cigarettes and shaking hands with them...I can't understand it after seeing the sights we have seen – men's eyes gorged out, ears cut off and some propped in doorways and burnt...[5]

In the locally published news sheet called 'Peninsula Press', the bearer of good news only, issue number forty-one, for Wednesday 30 June reported:

After special bombardment by French mortars, and while the bombardment of surrounding trenches was at its height, part of the Border Regiment, at the exact moment prescribed, leapt from their trenches as one man, like a pack of hounds streaming out of cover, raced across and took the work most brilliantly.

The 'Peninsula Press' was published daily from May 1915 by the GHQ Printing Section, Royal Engineers, in Imbros, until the last days of the campaign. The single sheet editions contained 'official news' propaganda informing the troops of local happenings at Gallipoli as well as how the War was progressing elsewhere. Another newssheet called the *Dardanelles Driveller* was also published. This was a lot more humorous, but sadly did not last very long.

Loss to the Borders was fairly light, largely thanks to the effective bombardment by the British 4.5-inch howitzers of 460/Battery and also the two French trench mortars, on loan from General Gouraud. These mortars, nicknamed *La Demoiselle*, could drop bombs ranging from thirty to seventy pounds of melinite vertically into the trenches at fairly short range. The British at this stage had only six 'Japanese' trench mortars. These arrived in mid-May 1915 from Japan, along with the instructions, but only printed in Japanese. There was a very limited supply of ammunition for these, and by early June 1915 Hamilton remarked that the War Office had let the stock of bombs run out because 'some ass has forgotten to order them in advance'. New bombs would have to be ordered from Japan, and it would be months before they arrived. This aside, of the six Japanese mortars, four were up at Anzac, leaving only two on the

A Japanese Trench Mortar, with no bombs ...*some ass has forgotten to order them in advance.* (© Chambers)

Helles front for the June attack. Howitzers were very scarce, but trench mortars were probably in greater demand than any other gun at this time.

The Capture of Boomerang Trench

Crouched down in the shelter of the trench,
While mortars shelled the way,
And naval might screamed thro' the air,
The Border fighters lay
In eager expectation, while
Red was their spirits sang,
For theirs the honour of the day –
To win the Boomerang!

Like pack of hounds they strained the leash,
And while commands rang out,
Like pack of hounds they raced to gain
The Boomerang Redoubt;
No chance the Turkish rifle fire
To stay their swift career
Across the hundred yards of scrub,
Or quell their frenzied cheer.

They swept the foe from parapet,
From round each maxim grim,
And hardly in their fury paused
When bullet touched a limb,
With butt and bayonet they slew
In onslaught none could face,
And cheered again, as in dismay
The foeman fled the place.

Tho' fierce the fight, so brief the same,
That they who watched behind
Scarce thought the thrilling deed was o'er
Its like seemed hard to find,
For when the Borders left their trench,
Few minutes scarce had run
Till their victorious shout proclaimed
The Boomerang was won.[6]

At 11:00 the artillery lengthened their fuse range to shell the ground beyond. On both sides of Gully Ravine the main party of assaulting troops scaled their stepladders and left their trenches to attack. The bombardment on Gully Spur had been so intense that the first two lines of Turkish trenches were virtually annihilated, leaving the occupants either dead or wounded. The main resistance on Gully Spur came from a machine gun on the right flank in the Boomerang. Even though the Borders had attacked fifteen minutes before the main assault, some elements of the Turkish garrison were still holding out in the redoubt and its satellites. This stubborn resistance inflicted a number of casualties on the 2/South Wales Borderers, who were attacking to the Borders left. This thorn did not stop them, and quickly the first few trenches were captured.

Sub-Lieutenant Frank Yeo, witnessed the SWB attack at 11:00:

> One place a little in advance of the Turkish trench was a sort of redoubt with several machine guns and from which the Turks threw bombs into our trenches – this was left for the South Wales Borderers to take. At 11 o'clock the SWB jumped over their trenches with fixed bayonets and charged the redoubt – it was dreadful to see them getting mowed down but a few reached the redoubt and then there was some battle!! You could see them sticking the Turks like pigs and the Turks putting up their hands and yelling 'Allah'!! They took the redoubt and about 80 prisoners...The SWB charge was great, they must have some pluck, if they are really Welshmen I take off my hat to them. Really our soldiers are wonders and you people in England can't do too much for them – the whole lot deserve VCs.[7]

With the exception of casualties here, the first two trench lines were taken with very little loss at all. Reverend Creighton, at the 89/Field Ambulance dressing station in Gully Ravine, wrote:

> ...soon the wounded started to pour in. First the slight cases able to walk, in crowds. Everything seemed to be going well. The Turks were on the run and we had got a line or two of trenches. Then later on in came the stretcher cases, and they kept coming all night and the next day.[8]

Hamilton had come over from Imbros in the destroyer HMS *Colne* for the battle, observing:

> The cliff line and half a mile inland is shrouded in a pall of yellow dust, which, as it twirls, twists and eddies, blots out Achi Baba himself. Through this curtain appear, dozens at a time, little balls of white – the shrapnel searching out the communication trenches and cutting the wire entanglements. At other times spouts of green or black vapour rise, mix and lose themselves in the yellow cloud. The noise is like the rumbling of an express train –continuous; no break at all.

87

Watching the men advancing, with the tin triangles on their backs, Hamilton went on to say:

> *The spectacle was extraordinary. From my post I could follow the movements of every man. One moment after 11 a.m. the smoke pall lifted and moved slowly on with a thousand sparkles of light in its wake: as if someone had quite suddenly flung a big handful of diamonds on to the landscape.*

Owing to the lesser bombardment east of Gully Ravine, the attack along Fir Tree Spur did not go as well, with casualties quickly mounting. The Official History said:

> *...the Turks had probably suffered less from the British fire than the attacking troops waiting in the trenches had suffered from the Turkish counter-bombardments.*

The bombardment on the line opposite the 4 and 7/Royal Scots did appear to achieve a fair degree of destruction, but nothing like as great as that to their left on Gully Spur:

> *The sun, high in the heavens by 9.am, but after thirty minutes' bombardment its golden disc was veiled by thick clouds of smoke and dust that floated skywards, while the acrid smell of powder hung heavily in the air.*

Second Lieutenant L. R. Grant, 4/Royal Scots wrote:

> *The minutes passed and we looked anxiously at our watches. The men were all standing ready with bayonets fixed at five minutes to eleven. Excitement ran high and a certain tense nervousness. It was the supreme test of all our months of training. Would we stand the test? Three minutes more, two minutes more. The rattle of the rifle fire had become more pronounced and bullets were smacking on the parapet and hissing over our heads.'One minute more, boys' then 'over you go lads' and with a yell that thrilled the very marrow in one's bones, the men hurled themselves over the parapet and dashed forward into the inferno of flame and smoke, bursting shells and zipping bullets.*[9]

Edinburgh's finest. Men of 4/Royal Scots before departing for Gallipoli.

Back Row: Lieut.Byers, Lieut. J M Slater, Lieut. J Riddell, Lieut. A Young, Lieut. R D Macrorie, Lieut, T D Aitchison, *Middle Row*: Dr Ewing, Lieut. F B Mackenzie, Lieut. J. Logan, Capt, J D Pollock, Lieut, C F Allan, Capt, J Robertson, Lieut. R E Mackie, Lieut. L R Grant, Lieut. J Morham, Lieut. J Gray, Capt. Pirie Watson. *Front Row*: Capt. G M'Crae, Capt. W C C Sinclair, Major J N Henderson, Major J Gray, Colonel Younger, Major Simson, Capt. J K M Hamilton, Capt A smith, Capt G A S Ross.
Absent: Lieut.-Col. S R Dunn. Capt. R W G Rutherford, Lieut.. P F Considine, Lieut. J Fleck, 2nd Lieut. W J Johnstone, Lieut. D M Stewart, 2nd Lieut C Paterson, 2nd Lieut. R J Gibson.

Officers of 4/Royal Scots. (© Chambers)

Back Row: Lieut. J A Young, Lieut. E J Thomson, 2nd Lieut. D Lyell, Lieut. J Ballantyne, Lieut. J C Bell, 2nd Lieut. N G Salvesen, 2nd Lieut. F W Thomson, Lieut. W C M'Geachin. *Middle Row*: 2nd Lieut. T M'Clelland, Lieut., C R Salvesen, Lieut. A O Cushny, Lieut. W R Kermack, Capt. A J Wightman, Capt. J A Torrance, Capt. W T Ewing, Capt J. M. Mitchell, Capt. J R Peebles, Lieut. N C Riddell, Capt. G G Weir. Front Row: Capt. A M Mitchell, Major J D Hamilton, Capt. J G P Romanes (Adjutant), Lieut.-Col. W Carmichael Peebles, T D The Right Hon. The Earl of Rosebery, KG, KT, VD, Hon. Colonel, Major A W Sanderson, Lieut.-Col. J Mill, VD, RAMC, Capt. J D Dawson, Capt D Clark. *Sitting:* Lieut. G W Hawes, Lieut A S Elliott, 2nd Lieut. T G Clark, Lieut. R M Galloway.

Officers of 7/Royal Scots, April 1915. (© Chambers)

89

At zero hour the Royal Scots leapt forward with great zeal and gallantly charged as:

> *...the storm beat upon them; a rain of missiles smote their ranks, but slanting their bodies to the blast the survivors dashed on without flinching through the smoke and flame.*

Out of this inferno they managed to capture both the first and second Turkish lines. At the sight of this determined advance, many of the Turks in the front trenches bolted, and those left were quickly dispatched with 'cold steel' in the mêlée that followed. Lieutenant F. B. Mackenzie tells how,

> *the Turks lucky enough to survive the charge should always remember the name of Royal Scot.*

The losses to the Scots were appalling, many of the casualties being inflicted by an undetected machine gun nest towards the position of H.13 on the Scots' extreme right. Second Lieutenant L. R. Grant concluded the entry in his diary that day with: 'over the remainder of that day it were perhaps better to draw a veil'. This Edinburgh sacrifice cost the lives of many good officers and men,

Captain George McCrae, 4/Royal Scots, aged thirty-one years, was wounded in the leg in the attack, but continued leading his men towards the Turkish trenches until killed by a gunshot to the head. He is commemorated on the Helles Memorial (Panels 26-30).

Lieutenant-Colonel S. R. Dunn, Commanding Officer, 4/Royal Scots. Mortally wounded in the attack on H.12a, he later died on a hospital ship and was buried at sea.

The Royal Scots panel on the Helles Memorial to the missing. (© Chambers)

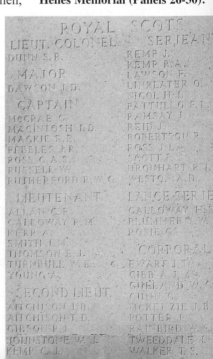

including Lieutenant-Colonel Spottiswoode Robert Dunn, T.D., 4/Royal Scots Commanding Officer. Dunn was mortally wounded just before reaching the first objective of H12a, falling between the British and Turkish lines. The majority of the other officers and men fell in this killing ground too. Sadly he died later on a hospital ship, aged fifty-two, and was buried at sea the following day:

As a soldier and a man he was worshipped by the whole battalion; he possessed that charm of manner that irresistibly sweeps up loyalty and love, and at his word officers and men would proudly have gone through any ordeal.

Piper-Major Andrew Buchan was another casualty as he advanced through No Man's Land:

...rifle in hand, continued to encourage forward a party of young Royal Scots, although he had twice been wounded. Hit for the third time, he fell dead on the parapet of the first Turkish trench.[10]

Both men are today commemorated on the Helles Memorial to the Missing.

Second-Lieutenant L. R. Grant was soon wounded, but a small party under Company-Sergeant-Major D. M. Lowe, 'C' Company, 4/Royal Scots, advanced a further hundred yards to the final objective, the second trench line at H.12, later to be known as the Eastern Birdcage. His party of about sixty men came under heavy enfilade fire from the western banks of Gully Ravine and the Nullah, owing to his party getting ahead of the 87 Brigade advance on the left. However the quick dash took the Turks completely by surprise, enabling the attackers to capture this last position successfully. From this vantage point Lowe's men poured heavy fire into the retreating Turks retiring up the gully. The ravine at this point was like the depression of a shallow saucer, with little cover to offer anybody who should pass through. In front of Lowe's party no more Turkish trenches were observed, only the summit of a small ridge, behind which, nobody knew what lay. The party was too small to exploit the situation further, so they quickly set about consolidating their gains.[11]

To the right of Lowe's position, where the ground was slightly higher, Lieutenant F. B. MacKenzie, 4/Royal Scots,[2] quickly set up his machine gun as defence for this section of trench. After he was seriously wounded, shot through the neck by a sniper, Sergeant John Gunn took up the gun position. With lack of shell, machine-guns were the only real support on Fir Tree Spur. To the right of 4/Royal Scots were 7/Royal Scots, who were successful in capturing part of H.12a.

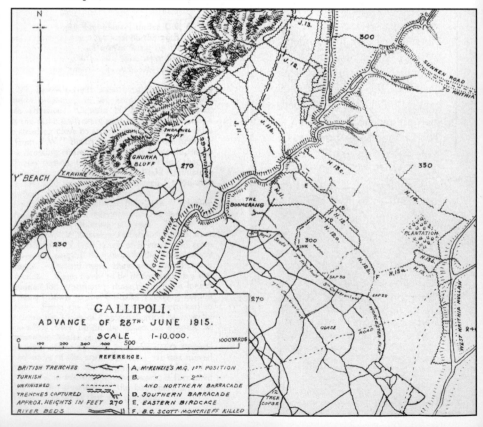

ZIG-ZAG

BOOMERANG

BRITISH FRONT LINE

Panoramic cross-section view of the ground where 4 and 7/Royal Scots attacked. (© Chambers)

When the 8/Highland Light Infantry Company came up in support, 7/Royal Scots moved on to attack H.12, the next trench beyond. The journal of Private William Begbie, 'C' Company, 7/Royal Scots describes that attack:

> [After] *a short halt during which the supporting waves closed up, the advance on the final objective was begun. By this time the Turks, having recovered from their panic, delivered such a terrific fire that our Company fell in bundles. Halfway across*

Map 13. Advance of 28 June 1915.

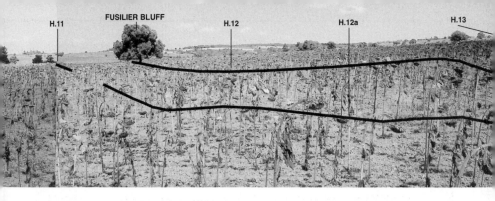

Major Sanderson dropped and Captain Dawson and Lieutenant Thomson were killed as they neared their goal. By now men were falling on my left and right. I then felt as if a horse had kicked my right thigh. I fell and when I got up I had no feeling in my leg so I fell again. When I felt where the pain was I saw my hand was covered with blood. When I started to move I heard bullets striking the ground. I lay still. I did not feel very much pain, but the sun high in the sky threw down intense heat on the sand, which was crawling with insects of every shape and size. The worst thing was the craving for water – mouths were so parched by heat and sand that tongues swelled. From the time we left our trench the enemy bombarded us with everything they had. When I fell for the second time I must have turned my arm because I found I was lying on my rifle with the butt about a foot from the front of my head. I was wondering what would be the best thing to do when I felt the rifle rocking and when I looked up I saw the butt had a piece of shrapnel embedded in it. I turned around and crawled back passing men of our Company, some dead, and some with ghastly wounds were obviously dying.[13]

The attack was so determined that again the Turks fled before this rush of men. The left section of H.12 was now completely captured, but further along the line the Turks still held firmly on.

On the Royal Scots' right, where the 8/Cameronians (Scottish Rifles) went forward, the situation was the worst thus far. The artillery barrage contained no high explosives, just shrapnel, so little or no damage was done to the Turkish lines. Men in the line quickly noticed that the majority of the shelling fell on the trenches to their left, in front of 87 Brigade on Gully Spur, with precious little falling on the Turks in front of them. An anonymous officer eyewitness observed:

...during the bombardment not one shell fell on the objective on the right of the 156th Brigade, and not more than six on the left.[13]

A hail of deadly frontal fire from trench H.12 met the first wave of the Cameronians, made worse from enfilade fire brought to bear from the

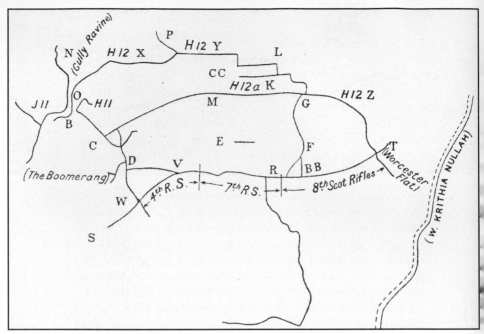

Map 14. 156 Brigade action of the 28 June 1915

undetected machine-gun nest in trench H.13, estimated to contain from six to eight machine guns. With the enemy barrage continuing, 'the sickening cough'[15] of the machine guns now lashed at the British parapets. The leading ranks were mown down, ripped to shreds, as soon as they left the cover of their trenches. There was no hesitation on part of the Cameronians, the second and third lines meeting the same fate, many of the third line falling even before they reached their own firing line:

> All ranks were slaughtered, literally by platoons...in a few minutes nothing was left of the battalion but one officer and a few men who dribbled back to their own line...

Within five minutes, the 8/Cameronians lost twenty-five officers out

View from the British front line where 7 and 8/Cameronians attacked.
(© Chambers)

of twenty-six and 448 men, more than 300 of which had been killed. The 7/Cameronians had only two companies in the same attack, and were devastated, losing fourteen officers and 258 men, with more than 150 killed. The 52nd Division History said:

> There was not the slightest hesitation on the part of any battalion...a perfect storm of machine-gun and rifle-fire burst on them, the bullets whipping up the dust and the Turkish shrapnel coming down like hail. The ground to be crossed was rough going but nearly flat, and the troops were exposed to view and fire from the moment they went over the parapet.[16]

Lieutenant Hew McCowan, 8/Cameronians (Scottish Rifles), was reported missing on 28 June 1915, and it was not until May 1916 that proof of his death was forthcoming. An officer of Hawke Battalion, RND, had taken a pair of field glasses and a revolver holster from a body lying on the field of battle. The field glasses were lost during the evacuation, but the holster was brought home and identified as having belonged to Lieutenant McCowan. He is commemorated on the Helles Memorial Panels 92-97).

On the extreme left some men did in fact reach the Turkish front line, 175 yards away, near the Royal Scots, where the lie of the land afforded more protection from the H.13 machine guns. Here a small ridge jutted out diagonally into No Man's Land, from the centre of 7/Royal Scots line, up the gentle slope northwards towards the Turkish trenches. From it the land fell away into Gully Ravine to the west. On the right of this ridge the whole of the ground crossed by 8/Cameronians was devoid of cover. The small party of Cameronians in the Turkish trench joined up with the 7/Royal Scots and begun to consolidate their bravely won position as best they could. Clinging tenaciously to their small part of H.12a, they waited for support. The attack elsewhere along this line had come to a complete standstill. No more men remained to

commemorated on the Helles Memorial (Panel 92-97). Many others whose names go unrecorded displayed similar acts of heroism, saving many of the wounded from a horrific death.

At 11:47 General de Lisle sent the following order to 156 Brigade that 'H.12 is to be taken at all cost. If necessary you will send forward your reserve battalion'. At this stage de Lisle, unaware of the attack's failure at this point and of the heavy casualties that the Cameronians had taken, did not realise the seriousness of the situation that faced 156 Brigade. On receiving these orders Brigadier-General Scott-Moncrieff ordered the last two companies of the 7/Cameronians (Scottish Rifles) from reserve to renew the attack. However, without artillery support this daylight attack would again be sheer murder, and his men probably knew that. Brigadier-General Scott-Moncrieff went forward to see the situation for himself, telling his Brigade-Major that he would be back in half-an-hour. Observing that some elements of the previous assaults had reached the Turkish Front line in H.12a opposite the 'Kink' (named from a sharp bend in the line), he ordered the last two companies of his brigade to advance in support of them against the right of H.12a. Two saps ran forward from the British line towards the enemy trenches, Sap No.29 on the right and Sap No.30 on the left. Both of these saps were now choked with dead and wounded but provided the only cover in that area. The saps were only shallow, but any advance over the top on the flat ground had already proved futile. The last of the Cameronians, stumbling over piles of dead and dying, moved up through the narrow communication trenches as fast as they could. At about 12:30 they went over the top, to be met by a hail of bullets as soon as they emerged from cover. Scott-Moncrieff had joined a small party of 7/Cameronians that had gathered at Sap 29. As the General emerged from this position he was immediately shot through the head, falling in No Man's Land. Lieutenant-Colonel John Boyd Wilson, the Cameronians' Commanding Officer, and his men tried to continue an advance as best they could, but the Turks had marked both these sap positions and as soon as anyone emerged they became immediate casualties, including Wilson who was killed. Getting no further forward than the two saps, the men were ordered to withdraw. Futile attacks by weakened territorial battalions, with no artillery

Found on the battlefield - the metal dog tag of 18 year old John Cubie, 1863, 7/Cameronians (Scottish Rifles) who was killed on 28 June 1915. He is today commemorated on the Helles Memorial to the Missing. (© Chambers)

support, were not the answer against the determined and firmly entrenched Turks. The Cameronians had suffered very heavily, including the loss of both their Commanding Officer and Brigade Commander. Brigadier-General Scott-Moncrieff probably knew that this last attack, like all the others before, did not stand even a slim chance of success. As the Divisional history says:

...those who know him best think that for this reason he intended to place himself in order to lead the men in person...it was his duty to order his men into the hurricane of fire, and it is certain that he, noble and sensitive man that he was, wished to take the same risks as his men.[18]

Brigadier-General W. Scott-Moncrieff, was killed in action during the afternoon of 28 June. Born in June 1858, he was educated at Wimbledon School and then the Royal Military College, Sandhurst. He was commissioned in the 57th Foot in May 1878, and with the Middlesex Regiment he later saw service in the Zulu War in 1879. During the Boer War he was severely wounded in the leg at Spion Kop, which left him slightly lame. When war broke out in August 1914 he came out of retirement, returning as a temporary Brigadier-General. In January 1915 he accepted command of 156 Brigade of the 52nd (Lowland) Division. He is today commemorated on Special Memorial C. 132 in Twelve Tree Copse Cemetery.

Some corner of a foreign field – Cameronian graves in Twelve Tree Copse Cemetery. (© Chambers)

The front line at Fusilier Bluff.

The elements of the Cameronians that had taken H.12a set about consolidating their gains as quickly as possible. Seeing that the advance on their right had failed, a sandbag block, later known as Southern Barricade, was hastily built across the captured trench. A further barricade, that was to become known as Northern Barricade, was constructed along trench H.12:

> *The dust and sand that filled the air clogged the rifle-bolts, while the men were suffering from exhaustion and the terrific mental strain of their first fight; their mouths were so parched by heat and dust that their tongues swelled and they could scarcely swallow the rations that they had carried up; worst of all was the craving for water, and the troops endured long hours of agony before the precious liquid could be sent to them.*

Whilst the above was taking place east of the ravine, the attack over on Gully Spur continued to go as planned. By noon, just before the Cameronians had gone over the top, 2/Royal Fusiliers had taken the final objectives of J.12 and J.13. The Gurkhas to the left of the Royal Fusiliers had cleared J.11a and were in occupation of the spur running down to the sea just in front of J.13; the point was later known as Fusilier Bluff. In Gully Ravine itself, 1/Lancashire Fusiliers were moving successfully along its western banks in order to join up the line with 156 Brigade in H.12.

Sub-Lieutenant Frank Yeo recalled:

> *We bagged a lot of Turks with our guns as they were*

Panoramic from Fusilier Bluff (Fifth Avenue), the furthest point of the British advance on Gully Spur. (© Chambers)

NULLAH

BRITISH FRONT LINE (FIFTH AVENUE)

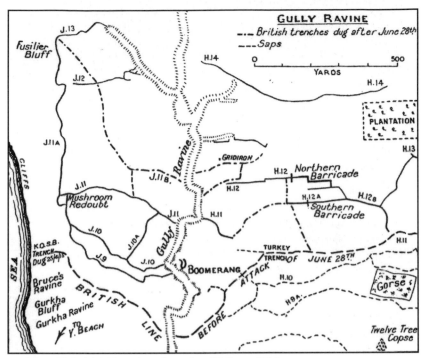

Map 15. British Trenches dug after 28 June 1915.

retreating. Unfortunately out of the four men I have with my gun I have already lost two in a few hours, one killed[19] and one wounded in the shoulder. I had a narrow shave when the bullet that killed my No.2 just grazed the gun I was firing at the time. It went over my shoulder and hit my man who was looking over it. It covered me with dirt and some got in my eye. I wondered what had happened. We have several wounded in the trench here. Two R.F men are just beside me now, one has his leg shattered and I have given him some opium pills so he is now quite happy. The other is only slightly wounded...I expect the Turks will counter attack tonight and I ought to get some fine targets. This is better than blowing up pheasants at Holme Park...[20]

At 14:00 the Turks launched several fierce and determined bombing

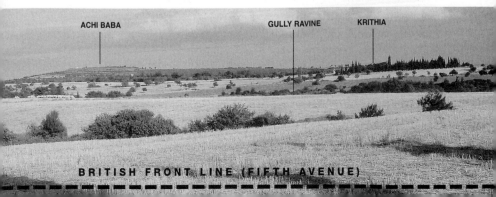

attacks, thrown against their lost positions near the gully on Fir Tree Spur and the eastern ends of the J trenches at the Nullah. At the Southern Barricade a Turkish bomb fell into the trench. Lance-Corporal A. Ross, 7/Cameronians, with no thought for his own safety, at once put his foot on it just as Private Young was leaning down to throw a coat over it. Throwing a coat over a bomb had a smothering affect that suppressed the explosion. The bomb exploded, wounding Ross terribly in the feet, legs, hands and face but he undoubtedly saved several lives by his self-sacrifice. He survived, both Cameronian men receiving the DCM for their gallantry.

Fusiliers returning from the trenches, June 1915. (IWM Q13315)

On Gully Spur, a large party approached towards the barricaded ravine shouting 'Lancashire Fusiliers!' and waving a white flag. This ruse by the Turks did not work, and they immediately attracted heavy fire, leaving over forty bodies behind. Bombs were an advantage the Turks had over the British. They had large quantities and put them to good use. Allied supplies were very small, and those that were available were used up very quickly. These local bomb attacks forced the British from the eastern halves of both J.12 and J.13 and also pushed back the majority of the Lancashire Fusiliers to the western bank of the gully. The Turks had not yet accepted defeat.

Two of the Lancashire Fusiliers amongst the 'six VCs before breakfast' were to become casualties as a result of these attacks, Lance-Sergeant William Keneally and Temporary Major Cuthbert Bromley.

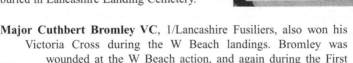

Lance-Sergeant William Stephen Keneally VC, 1/Lancashire Fusiliers, won his Victoria Cross during the landings on W Beach, 25 April 1915. He survived the fighting on the beaches and the three battles of Krithia. Promoted by this stage to Sergeant he was mortally wounded during the battle of Gully Ravine, dying on 29 June 1915, aged twenty-nine. News of his death did not reach his family until October 1915, long after they had celebrated his award of the Victoria Cross and were, with the local council, making plans to honour him further. He is buried in Lancashire Landing Cemetery.

Major Cuthbert Bromley VC, 1/Lancashire Fusiliers, also won his Victoria Cross during the W Beach landings. Bromley was wounded at the W Beach action, and again during the First Battle of Krithia, when he was hospitalised. Returning to his regiment on 17 May he saw further action during the Third Battle of Krithia in early June. When the CO of the 1/Lancashire Fusiliers fell ill, he took command of the Battalion in what was to be his last action on the Peninsula, the Battle of Gully Ravine. After giving his men a 'stirring address, which was warmly applauded', he led them over the top, being wounded in the heel almost immediately. He refused to leave his men, and was reported seen using two Turkish rifles as crutches and stumbling on with his men. Later he ordered two stretcher-bearers to carry him, but insisted that he would go to hospital

103

only after the line had been consolidated that night. Evacuated from Gallipoli to Egypt for treatment, he began his return journey on the transport ship *Royal Edward*. This ship was torpedoed and sunk on 13 August. Bromley was a powerfully built man and a splendid gymnast and swimmer. He seemed to have initially survived the sinking, and was reported swimming in the water when a rescue boat or a piece of debris accidentally collided with him, knocking him out and thus drowning. Reverend Creighton wrote of him:

He had an absolutely cool head and never seemed in the least perturbed or worried, and saw to everything himself...in my opinion he was one of the finest soldiers in the Division.[21]

He is today commemorated on the Helles Memorial (Panel 218).

About 18:00, 5/Gurkha and 1/Royal Munster Fusiliers were ordered to retake the lost portions of J.12 and J.13. Although this was eventually done after much hand-to-hand fighting and bombing, by nightfall the Turks had counter-attacked again, and recaptured both eastern ends of the trenches. During the time of the Gurkha and Munster attack, the 1/Royal Dublin Fusiliers were ordered up from reserve in Geoghegan's Bluff to the barricade made by the 1/Border Regiment, later called Border Barricade. They then advanced up the Gully towards the Nullah and the eastern end of trench J.12. Heavy fire met the Dublins, who made little progress. They did try digging a trench on the western side of the ravine to connect to J.12, but fierce Turkish opposition forced them back to the line at J.11a. Lieutenant O'Hara of the 1/Royal Dublin Fusiliers writes that we were in a condition bordering on lunacy when it was all over. The Munster history describes how the men were in a very bad state from exhaustion and want of water and food, after thirty-six hours of fighting and digging. Many literally collapsed, finding it difficult even to get out of the trenches without help.

Lieutenant Lawrence Clive Boustead, 1/Royal Dublin Fusiliers. He was present at the River Clyde landing on V Beach, being wounded in the cheek the following day whilst storming Sedd-el-Bahr fort. He was evacuated to hospital at Malta, rejoining his battalion at the beginning of June. In the early hours of June 29, during one of three night attacks made by the Turks, 'after doing excellent work under very trying circumstances, and whilst encouraging and keeping his men together', wrote his Commanding Officers, he was killed, aged twenty-one years. He was originally buried in Geoghegan's Bluff, also known as 'G' Bluff, but after the war his remains were moved to plot VII, row B, grave 3, in the Geoghegan's Bluff Plot in Twelve Tree Copse Cemetery.

Second Lieutenant Herbert George Rogers, 9/Somerset Light Infantry, attached to 1/Royal Dublin Fusiliers. He was killed on 29 June 1915, aged twenty-four. A friend and fellow officer wrote with reference to the circumstances of his death:

'I expect Herbert told you what a hard job he had the other night in that sap when he was attacked from three sides at once...Everyone said he was wonderful that night, as he practically did the whole thing, and could not even get any support from the other companies. I expect by the time you get this you will have heard of the advance made by us and the Indian Brigade on the left on June 28th. About 2.30 I was sent off on a job with forty men and it was not till about 3 a.m. next morning, June 29th, that I got back to my own Battalion...To my great relief Herbert was then all right...I went back to where he was and lay down behind him, as there was no room for both of us in the little trench they had dug, and he told me what had been happening and what an awful time they had had. It was light now, but there was still a heavy fire; apparently it was the nullah again that caused the trouble. The trenches on the right and left of the nullah were taken all right, but the troops which were suppose to swing round and connect the two across the nullah were unable to do so, and our Battalion was ordered to do this, and although it was dark and they were met by the enemy in far greater numbers than had been expected, they forced them back and, whilst being constantly attacked, dug themselves in where I found them. Herbert must have done very well, though he did not tell me so himself. Well, we were talking like this when he stood up to fire and direct his men, and fell down beside me wounded...He died about one hour and a half afterwards...When he fell I never thought it would be fatal, as he talked to me in quite his natural voice and did not seem to be in any pain. ...I did not dare leave the firing line myself, as I was the only officer in that part of the line now, but as luck would have it my servant was quite close, so we lifted him up on his back and the brave fellow carried him right back along the firing line till he was stopped by some of our men who said that if he went any further they would only both get killed as they were being very badly enfiladed at this point; so he made him comfortable in a little hollow in the ground where he would be safe, and himself went on and brought back some fresh water. Herbert thanked him again and again for all he did for him – in fact, that was all he spoke about and that was so like Herbert, so thoughtful and kind and so bright to the very last, and when the end came he merely seemed to drop off to sleep...My servant has been to-day and saw his body buried close to where he died so bravely...and I will see a cross is put up to mark the spot.

His grave was later lost, so he is today commemorated on the Helles Memorial (Panels 190-196).

General de Lisle had put the command of 156 Brigade, after Brigadier-

General Scott-Moncrieff's death, in the hands of Lieutenant-Colonel Cayley of 88 Brigade. In the late afternoon, supported by only a few guns, 1/Essex and 5/Royal Scots tried a fresh assault on H.12, but this again proved impossible, meeting with the same result as suffered by 156 Brigade. The Turks were expecting the attack to be renewed, and thus maintained heavy shelling on the British lines. Not a single person reached H.12, all being cut down immediately after leaving the cover of the trenches. Incredibly, a further attempt was made towards the evening, but this fared no better. Turkish fire was accurately directed from trenches still untouched by British artillery. After dark the 2/Hampshire Regiment began relieving the Royal Scots and the Cameronians in the western end of H.12 and H.12a. This proved a difficult and confusing process as the narrow trenches were still littered with the dead, dying and debris from the morning's battle. During this relief the Turks made two fierce counter-attacks on the line. Hamilton awoke about midnight during the time of his attack and wrote:

> *...far away I could see faint corruscation of sparks; star*

A drawing, depicting part of the action that earned Second Lieutenant Herbert James, 4/Worcestershire Regiment, the VC. He is seen leading a mix of men forward, mainly 5/Royal Scots in a failed attempt to capture H.12 on 28 June.

shells; coloured fire balls from pistols; searchlights playing up and down the coast.

Both of these attacks were repulsed with heavy loss to the Turks. When dawn came, the relief complete, the front of the line had a new carpet of dead. 156 Brigade was now fully relieved and in the reserve trenches near Twelve Tree Copse.

The Turkish trenches at H.12 and H.12a on the right remained in the Turks' possession for the rest of the campaign, as did the Nullah and eastern ends of J.12 and J.13.

The wounded lay where they had fallen in No Man's Land, the trenches and the saps. Many were in exposed positions so could not be rescued until nightfall; many would not live that long. They were not only exposed to the enemy, but also to the scorching sun that was likened to a 'blazing death star', an enemy crueller than the Turk. It was not long until the scrub and sun-browned grass caught fire again, devouring anything in its path. Those wounded who were helpless perished, burnt to death in the blaze. A blood red sunset closed a bloody day, and night came mercifully to cloak the scene of horror,

Sub-Lieutenant Frank Yeo wrote of the conditions after the day's battle:

The Turks have left everything behind them, rifles, ammunition, water bottles, etc. The place is covered with dead and wounded...The General has just sent up to congratulate our lads and they deserve it. The Turks must have thought they were going to hold the position for years I should think. They have beautiful dugouts, made with roofs etc. As I write they have started their 'Hymn of Hate', shrapnel coming down in bucketfuls, but I don't think they will move us.[22]

The following message was received by Major-General Granville Egerton, G.O.C, 52nd Division, dated 29 June, congratulating the troops:

General de Lisle wishes to express how much he valued the help given to the 29th Division in yesterday's attack by the 156th Brigade. The attack by the 156th Brigade was almost entirely successful – the 4th and 7th Royal Scots succeeded in every detail in the task imposed upon them. The 8th Scottish Rifles met with enormous resistance owing to the fact that our artillery had not prepared the Turkish position in front of them quite so successfully as in other places. The 8th Scottish Rifles were gallantly led. This position was unsuccessfully attacked twice by the 88th Brigade (29th Division) with great gallantry. General de Lisle does not blame the 8th Scottish Rifles at all for their failure.

He much regrets the death of Brigadier General Scott-Moncrieff.
Egerton, who was powerless to intervene as his men during this action
were under the command of de Lisle, was heartbroken to see the
destruction of his brigade. He was also furious to hear Hunter-Weston's
comment of being delighted to hear that the pups had been so well
blooded. The losses by both battalions of the Cameronians were so
severe that after this battle, on 1 July, they were forced to form a
composite battalion of the 7/8 Cameronians, containing only three
companies of the survivors. Likewise the 4/Royal Scots and the
7/Royal Scots, who were equally devastated by the heavy losses during
the recent battle, were obliged to amalgamate on 7 July. The 5/Royal
Scots, after only two months of fighting, had dwindled to less than one
company. The 29th Division, at this time, had become only a remnant
of the proud division it was a couple months previously.

1. The Royal Naval Armoured Car Division, (Royal Naval Air Service) was an unusual unit attached to the infantry as dismounted machine-gun units. Their armoured cars failed to make an impression when used during the Third Battle of Krithia. See *The Gallipolian*, No.96, Autumn 2001, pp.42-54.
2. 'My Gallipoli Story' by Sgt. S. Evans, 1/Border Regiment, *The Gallipolian*, No.46, Christmas 1984, p.20.
3. *Diary kept by the Officers of 'C' Company, 4th Battalion The Royal Scots (Queen's Edinburgh Rifles) during their journey to and stay on the Gallipoli Peninsula May and June 1915.* This was written by Captain R.W.G. Rutherford, killed 28 June, and 2/Lt. L.R.Grant.
4. Also known as 'Turkey Trot', 'The Turkey' or 'Turkish Trench'
5. 'Letters from Frank, European War', August 4th, 1914, *The Gallipolian*, No.57, Autumn 1988, p.18.
6. *Stray Shots from the Dardanelles*, A collection by Lance Corporal W F Rollo dedicated to All Ranks of the 1st Battalion the Border, Regiment, *The Gallipolian*, No.46, Christmas 1984, p.17.
7. 'Letters from Frank, European War', August 4th, 1914, *The Gallipolian*, No.57, Autumn 1988, p.16.
8. Creighton, Reverend Oswin, CF, *With the Twenty Ninth Division in Gallipoli: A Chaplain's Experience,* (1916), p.146.
9. *Diary kept by the Officers of 'C' Company, 4th Battalion The Royal Scots (Queen's Edinburgh Rifles) during their journey to and stay on the Gallipoli Peninsula May and June 1915.*
10. Thompson, R. R., Lieutenant-Colonel, *The Fifty-Second (Lowland) Division 1914-1918*, (1923), p.53
11. Lowe was awarded the DCM for this action.
12. MacKenzie was awarded the MC for this action.
13. A memoir transcribed by Mrs.Begbie from the journal of her husband, Private William Begbie of "C" Company,1/7th Royal Scots. Major Sanderson, Major Dawson and Lieutenant Thomson are commemorated on the Helles Memorial.
14. Thompson, *Op.Cit.*, (1923), p.52.
15. Ibid., p.57.
16. Ibid., p.53.
17. Creighton, *Op.Cit.,* (1916), p.146.
18. Thompson, *Op.Cit.,* (1923), pp.60-61.
19. Petty Officer Mechanic R. R. Thomas, buried in Twelve Tree Copse Cemetery.
20. Letters from Frank, *Op.Cit.,* No.57, Autumn 1988, p.18.
21. Creighton, *Op.Cit.,* (1916), pp.149-150.
22. Letters from Frank, *Op.Cit.,* No.57, Autumn 1988, p.19.

Chapter Five

THE AFTERMATH

The Turks were extremely worried at this stage, as the advance along Gully Spur had seriously enfiladed their positions on the eastern banks of Gully Ravine. Five lines of trenches were lost and now Krithia was in grave danger of being lost too. The Turks began a new series of desperate counter-attacks to win back their lost territory and make good their bad position.

During the night of 30 June, two Turkish Regiments crept along the cliff tops to the northernmost British positions at Fusilier Bluff. The Turkish masses were soon detected by the searchlights of HMS *Scorpion*, whose guns decimated their advance in minutes. When dawn came all that remained in front of the trenches were 300 dead Turkish bodies, and 180 prisoners belonging to the 13th, 16th and 33rd Regiments who were captured when they were found hiding out in the scrub.

By the morning of the 30 June the Gurkhas (5 and 6/Gurkha Battalions) had finally secured the western end of J.13, after this section of the trench had changed hands several times during the previous couple of days. During the night of 30 June the Turks made a bomb attack from the direction of the Nullah on the Gurkhas in J.13. The Gurkhas, having no bombs, were forced back, but a determined counter attack with kukris, led by Lieutenant-Colonel the Hon. C. G. Bruce, succeeded in regaining a small but important footing in the line. Bruce however, ended up severely wounded in both legs.

The following night, 1 July, after it had started to rain, another Turkish attack was launched, this time against 10/Gurkha in J.12 and a partly finished trench (to become known as Inniskilling Inch), held by the 1/Royal Inniskilling Fusiliers, that ran south from the barricade in

Fusilier Bluff from the site of the Turkish Trenches. The shallow dip of the mine crater dates from October 1915. (© Chambers)

British trenches at Fusilier Bluff. (IWM Q14851)

Map 16. Gurkha Operations from 28 June to 5 July 1915

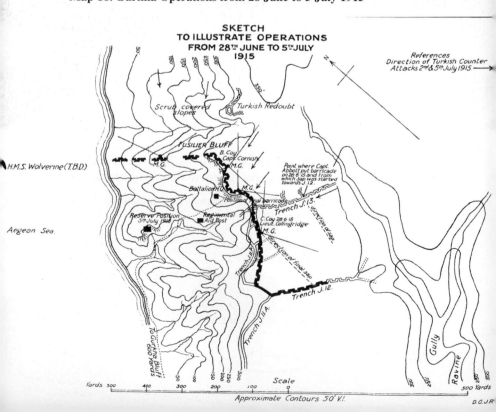

SKETCH
TO ILLUSTRATE OPERATIONS
FROM 28TH JUNE TO 5TH JULY
1915

References
Direction of Turkish Counter
Attacks 2nd & 5th July 1915 ⟶

Scrub covered slopes

Turkish Redoubt

FUSILIER BLUFF

B. Coy
Capt Cornish
M.G.

M.G.

H.M.S. Wolverine (T.B.D.)

Point where Capt.
Abbott put barricade
on 28·6·15 and from
which sap was started
towards J.12.

Battalion H.Q.

Position of final barricade

Trench J.13.

direction of sap.

Reserve Position
5th July 1915

Regimental
Aid Post

C Coy 28·6·15
Lieut. Collingridge
M.G.

Aegean Sea.

Direction of final sap

Trench J.13.

Trench J.II

Trench J.12.

Trench J.II.A.

Gully

Ravine

To Gurkha Bluff
600 Yards

Scale

Yards 500   400   300   200   100   0   500 Yards

Approximate Contours 50' V.I.

D.G.J.R.

British trench near Fusilier Bluff. (WSRC RSR PH 7/11)

J.12. Owing to lack of bombs, the troops were forced to give ground. Captain Gerald Robert O'Sullivan, with just over a company of Inniskillings and with bombing support from Corporal James Somers, restored the situation by recapturing the whole of J.12 as far as the Nullah just as the day broke. For gallantry in this action both O'Sullivan and Somers were awarded the Victoria Cross. Somers was also promoted in the field to sergeant. Unfortunately, owing to a misunderstanding, the men in J.12 then withdrew along the trench back to the old barricade, although under no pressure from the enemy. The Turks immediately seized the window of opportunity, reoccupying the now empty section of trench.

Captain Gerald Robert O'Sullivan.

Gerald Robert O'Sullivan was born on 8 November 1888 at Frankfield, Douglas, County Cork, son of Lieutenant-Colonel George Lidwell O'Sullivan and his wife Charlotte. He spent most of his boyhood in Dublin, entering Wimbledon College in 1899. When he left Wimbledon in June 1906 he entered the Royal Military College, Sandhurst, being commissioned on 9 May 1909 in the Royal Inniskilling Fusiliers as a Second-Lieutenant. He saw service in China, which included the revolution of 1911, and later in India with his battalion.

When war broke out in August 1914 the 1/Inniskillings were brought back to England to form part of 87 Brigade, 29th Division. The 29th Division sailed for Egypt in March 1915, landing in Gallipoli on 25 April 1915. O'Sullivan now commanded a company and fought many actions against the Turks in the Helles sector as the breakout from the beaches commenced. One such action was on the night of 18 June, when O'Sullivan organised an immediate counter-attack that drove the Turks out of the recently occupied Turkey Trench previously held by the 2/South Wales Borderers on the Inniskilling flank. (see pages 63-64).

In another action, during the night of 1 July 1915, the Turks attacked and captured trenches held by the Gurkhas after some very fierce hand to hand fighting, forcing the Gurkhas back. O'Sullivan led a counter-attack that regained the lost trenches, but was wounded in the leg during the action, being evacuated to hospital in Egypt. For this action, and the action of 18/19 June 1915, he received the Victoria Cross.

His citation appeared in the *London Gazette* of 1 September 1915:

For most conspicuous bravery during operations south west of Krithia, on the Gallipoli Peninsula. On the night of the 1st-2nd July, 1915, when it was essential that a portion of trench which had been lost should be regained, Captain O'Sullivan, although not belonging to the troops at this point, volunteered to lead a party of bomb throwers to effect the recapture. He advanced in the open under a very heavy fire, and in order to throw his bombs with greater effect, got up on the parapet, where he was completely exposed to the fire of the enemy occupying the trench. He was finally wounded, but not before his inspiring example had led on his party to make further efforts, which resulted in the recapture of the trench.

On the night of the 18/19 June, 1915, Captain O'Sullivan saved a critical situation in the same locality by his great personal gallantry and good leading.

O'Sullivan rejoined his regiment at Suvla on 11 August 1915. On 21 August O'Sullivan, during an attack on Hill 70, otherwise known as Scimitar Hill, was killed. Reported missing in action at first, and believed to be wounded, his body was never found. His VC was posthumously awarded. He is commemorated on the Helles Memorial (Panel 97).

Sergeant James Somers

James Somers was born at Belturbet, County Cavan, son of Robert and Charlotte Somers. He first joined the Special Reserve of the Royal Munster Fusiliers on 14 January 1913. He joined the 2/Royal Inniskilling Fusiliers in July 1914, and later served in Belgium and France when war broke out, being wounded at the Battle of Mons. After recovery from his wounds in England he was ordered to join the 1st Battalion, and sailed off to Gallipoli.

His citation appeared in the *London Gazette* of 1 September 1915:

For most conspicuous bravery on the night of 1-2 July 1915, in the southern zone of the Gallipoli Peninsula, when, owing to hostile bombing, some of our troops had retired from a sap, Sergeant Somers remained alone on the spot until a party brought up bombs. He then climbed over into the Turkish trench, and bombed the Turks with great effect. Later on, he advanced into the open under very heavy fire, and held back the enemy by throwing bombs into their flank until a barricade had been established. During this period he frequently ran to and from our trenches to obtain fresh supplies of bombs. By his great gallantry and coolness Sergeant Somers was largely instrumental in effecting the recapture of a portion of our trench, which had been lost.

A drawing of Somers winning his VC during the night of 1-2 July 1915.

Somers remained at Gallipoli until the close of the campaign, later seeing further service in France, taking part in the 1 July 1916 attack on the Somme at Beaumont Hamel. On the 1 April 1917 he joined the Army Service Corps. After being gassed quite badly, he was to die at his home in Cloughjordan, County Tipperary on 7 May 1918. He is buried in the churchyard at Modreemy, County Tipperary.

Second Lieutenant Herbert James, 4/Worcestershire Regiment, won his VC at Gully Ravine, 28 June and 2 July 1915.

Herbert James was born on 13 November 1888 in Ladywood, Birmingham, the son of Mr and Mrs Walter James, his father running a jewellery engraving business. After school Herbert joined the 21/Lancers as a trooper, and later the Worcestershire Regiment, seeing

A contemporary illustration of James winning his VC

service in Egypt and India before the war. After war was declared in 1914 he was commissioned into the 4/Worcestershire Regiment, leaving for the Dardanelles on 22 March 1915. He landed with his regiment at W Beach on 25 April, being wounded in the head the following day. Evacuated to Malta he returned later to see further action at Gallipoli, including the Battle of Gully Ravine. On 28 June, James was acting as a liaison officer to 5/Royal Scots.

His citation appeared in the *London Gazette* of 1 September 1915:

For most conspicuous bravery during the operations in the Southern Zone of the Gallipoli Peninsula. On 28 June, when a portion of the regiment had been checked, owing to all the officers being put out of action, Second Lieutenant James, who belonging to a neighbouring unit, entirely on his own initiative, gathered together a body of men and led them forward under heavy shell and rifle fire. He then returned, organised a second party and again advanced. His gallant example put fresh life into the attack. On 3 July [actually 2 July], in the same locality, Second Lieutenant James headed a party of bomb throwers up a Turkish communication trench and after nearly all his bomb throwers had been killed or wounded, he remained alone at the head of the trench and kept back the enemy single-handed until a barrier had been built behind him and the trench secured. He was throughout exposed to murderous fire.

James survived continued service on the Peninsula until the night of 27 September, when he was wounded in the foot at an advanced sap-head. Evacuated, he returned to England. He saw further action on the Western Front, including the Somme fighting of 1916, when he was wounded at the village of Contalmaison. He survived the war, dying in 1958.

Towards the evening of 2 July, the Turks attacked again, this time against the line at Fusilier Bluff and the western end of J.13, held by the Gurkhas and Inniskillings. At 16:00, after a wholly ineffective thirty-minute bombardment the Turks began to advance. From a northerly direction they came forward in swarms, across the open ground, some also advancing across the cliff tops and over the steep spurs that ran down to the sea. HMS *Scorpion*, lying off the coast, let loose her guns, along with every British machine gun and rifle that could be mustered. The fire decimated the Turks in less than 15 minutes, the survivors being forced back to the cover of the Nullah. An hour later the Turkish artillery again came into action, and just before dark about 1,800 Turks advanced, shoulder-to-shoulder, from the northern end of the Nullah. At first the Turkish commanders were observed to have great difficulty in getting their men to advance, as :

> the enemy's officers greatly distinguished themselves, waving their swords and running well out into the open to get the men forward.

They were decimated by 10/Battery RFA, which showed the power of its guns in defence when firing shrapnel. Some did get to within 40 yards of the British trenches, but were cut down by the scything effect of concentrated rifle and machine-gun fire. All that was left was a fresh carpet of dead. The history of 5/Gurkha describes:

> ...extraordinary scenes occurred in our own trenches, now so congested by the presence of the supports that many men were unable to find standing room at the parapet. Some of these overcame the difficulty by climbing onto the parados and shooting from there over the heads of their comrades in front. Others were seen to hand their rifles to their more fortunately placed friends, whose own weapons had become too hot to hold.

During the afternoon of 3 July the 14/Sikhs made an attempt to retake the eastern end of J.13. They succeeded in bombing out the Turks from the first barricade, but found a second barricade behind, which they could not take. Apart from continuous shelling, the Turkish activity during 3 and 4 July quietened down a little, giving time for everyone to recuperate.

It seemed that the Turks had given up all hope of recapturing their lost trenches, but although it was not known at the time, this was just the lull before the storm. So far the Turks had suffered enormous casualties and the threat of losing their Southern zone looked imminent. To reinforce the area, the Turks brought in three extra divisions during the evening of 3 July: the 5th Division from Anzac, the 4th Division from Bulair and the 3rd Division from Kum Kale. Giving themselves time to reorganise on 4 July, the morning of 5 July

Map 17. Trench Map after Gully Ravine battle, July 1915

116

was to witness a huge Turkish counter-attack, the biggest seen so far. The 3rd Division was to assault the J trenches, the 5th Division the H trenches, whilst the 4th Division was to be held in reserve. The attack was going to be extended along the whole southern sector by the other units already holding these positions. The Turkish attack needed to be successful at all costs, otherwise all looked close to lost for them. If the Helles front crumbled, the British would have an open field to advance, join up with the Anzac front and secure the Dardanelles.

After almost a two-day lull in the battle a heavy Turkish bombardment began early in the morning on 5 July, whilst still dark, taking the British completely by surprise. The Turks were soon observed massing for an attack, which prompted the British guns to throw down a counter-bombardment, concentrating on the Turkish trenches and the Nullah. HMS *Wolverine*, using her searchlight, was able to illuminate Turkish troops advancing across the cliff tops, and bombard them to a devastating effect. At about 04:15 the Turks began their attack, to be driven back with heavy loss as in the previous assaults. At about 06:00 the Turks again attacked, like a swarm of bees:

...thousands of Turks in a bunch, so the boys say, swarmed out of their trenches and the Gully Ravine. Well, they were stopped dead. They lie, still. The guns ate the life out of them.

British shrapnel and rifle fire had done it again; only about thirty Turks actually reached the British parapet. These attacks were far greater than any other experienced by the British:

Flares, shot up by our officers, showed the Turks advancing in regular parade formation in line of columns. As soon as the Turks saw that they had been observed, they charged, yelling their war cry: 'Allah, Allah!' The Gurkhas waited patiently, lining the trenches as thickly as they could stand. They allowed the Turks to approach within fifty yards of them and then opened such a hurricane of rifle and machine-gun fire that the Turks were absolutely crumpled up in ranks as they stood.[1]

On came the Turks, line after line, but not a single man reached the parapet of our front-line trench. They were literally mown to pieces, and the dead were heaped one on top of the other. The rifles of the men in the firing line became so hot that it was necessary to pass up rifles from the supports whilst the men in support kept the firing line rifles while they cooled and recharged the magazines.[2]

The Turkish attacks continued all over the southern zone, but by midday they had all exhausted themselves and failed, resulting in enormous Turkish casualties:

> *...line upon line of Turkish dead, silent witnesses to the terribly accurate fire poured into them...They are brave fellows, those Turks, and it was a sad sight to see so many gallant men laid low.*[3]

British losses were negligible.

The Turks officially admitted that their losses between 28 June and 5 July were over 16,000, with at least 10,000 being killed at Gully Ravine. These were heavier losses than the May 19 attack up at Anzac. Little *Mehmet* (the Turkish equivalent to 'Tommy Atkins') fought with a steadfast courage to defend his homeland from the invaders. This won him the respect of the Allied soldiers. The Turks actually stated that the battle of Zighin Dere, as they called it, was the most costly action they had yet fought on the Peninsula. The killing fields of Gully Ravine had taken their toll on both sides. Second-Lieutenant Savory, 14/Sikhs wrote:

> *By July 5th, the Indian Brigade had shot its bolt. All its four battalions had been decimated...we were no more than a band of survivors.*

This left the 14/Sikhs with little more than ninety men. This remnant

Turkish prisoners being marched through the gully, June 1915. (IWM Q13337)

was amalgamated with 10/Gurkha, who themselves had only a subaltern in command. 5/Gurkha and 6/Gurkha were in a like state, and were also combined.

The Turkish position was critical; the only men left in a fighting state were those of the 4th Division which had been held in reserve. If Hamilton could have renewed the attack at this stage he might well have broken through this flank. However, both British and Turkish were equally exhausted, and with lack of artillery support and further troops both sides had fought themselves to a stalemate.

Turkish morale had suffered terribly in this attack. A Turkish order by Colonel Rifaat Bey, Commander of the 11th Division, translated:

The Turkish wounded soldier statue at Morto Bay. (© Chambers)

There is nothing that causes us more sorrow, increases the courage of the enemy and encourages him to attack more freely, causing us great losses, than the losing of these trenches. Henceforth, commanders who surrender these trenches, from whatever side the attack may come before the last man is killed, will be punished in the same way as if they had run away...I hope that this will not occur again. I give notice that if it does, I shall carry out the punishment. I do not desire to see a blot made on the courage of our men by those who escape from the trenches to avoid the rifle and machine-gun fire of the enemy. Henceforth, I shall hold responsible all Officers who do not shoot with their revolvers all the privates who try to escape from the trenches on any pretext.

Colonel Hassan Lutli Bey of 127/Infantry Regiment added a further note to this, which also had the signatures of the company commanders of the battalion, which further stated:

To Commander of the 1st Battalion. The contents will be communicated to the officers and I promise to carry out the

Walking wounded passing through the gully on their way to the beach.
(IWM Q13329)

orders till the last drop of our blood has been shed.

On the morning of 7 July the Turks requested an armistice in order to bury their dead. A note was received, from a Turk bearing the flag of truce, which was addressed in a sealed envelope to the British Commander in Chief. The British answer was 'no'. It was believed at the time that the Turks were more worried about the effect the dead would have on the morale of their troops if ordered to attack over the bodies of their comrades, than humanitarian or health reasons. Reports

The Turkish Nuri Yamut Memorial at Fusilier Bluff. This commemorates the 10,000 Turkish martyrs who died during the battle at Gully Ravine. (©
Chambers)

show that the Turks tried again during the next couple of days to request a truce, but this was either ignored or answered with a hail of bullets. Sir Ian Hamilton remarked:

...dead Turks are better than barbed-wire, and so, though on grounds of humanity as well as health, I should like the poor chaps decently buried, I find myself forced to say No.

The conditions in the captured trenches and in the newly taken part of Gully Ravine were indescribably awful. Doctor William Ewing described it:

To the ordinary litter and filth to be expected where the Turks had been settled for weeks, were added the wreck and ruin wrought by the bombardment, the scattered remains of food, dishes, firewood, articles of clothing and kit, abandoned in the scurry and scramble of the flight before our bayonets. The mangled bodies of the dead, unburied, half-buried, or partially dug up by H.E. shells, under the fierce heat, with loathsome clouds of flies, could only be dealt with by fire. The valley with its heaps of rotting refuse, its burning pyres and sickening stench, was a veritable Gehenna.[4]

The burial parties had a dreadful experience trying to dispose of the dead. In this nauseating atmosphere they did the best they could in the

British troops resting in shelters captured from the Turks in Gully Ravine.
(IWM Q13345)

prevailing conditions. It was impossible to burn the bodies at first, given the risk of attracting enemy shellfire, so the bodies were buried as best they could be. Later they were collected together, soaked in petrol and set alight. Colonel G. H. Edington (1/Lowland Field Ambulance) remarked that:

> ...every here and there irregularities in the ground, covered with loose earth and sandbags, and giving off a horrible stench, marked where our men had buried Turkish dead.

Ashmead-Bartlett, who visited Gully Ravine after the battle, wrote:

> ...all the way up that portion of the gully, only 24 hours before in the enemy's possession, there is a litter of debris of the camp and of the great fight. Scattered bodies half protruding from the ground, hastily-dug graves, hundreds of rifles and bayonets, some broken, but the majority intact, thousands upon thousands of rounds of ammunition – we made a very big haul indeed in this last engagement – entrenching tools, loaves of bread, soldiers' packs, Turkish letters, a Mullah's prayer stool (a souvenir eagerly sought after), greatcoats and kits, blankets and old sacks, cooking utensils, and firewood, left just where the enemy abandoned them when our gallant infantry broke through

The spoils of war - captured Turkish rifles, ammunition and equipment, 29 June 1915. (IWM Q13334)

Cremating the Turkish dead after the Battle of Gully Ravine. (IWM Q13333)

*at the bayonet's point. Great fires burning at intervals. They are
avoided by all, and give forth a horrid, and sickly stench. On
these the Turkish dead, who have been hastily collected, are
being burnt, for it is all important to get the dead out of the way
as quickly as possible in this hot climate.*

The British casualties between the 28-30 June, although most were on
the first day, amounted to 3,800. 156 Brigade lost 1,353, nearly half its
total strength. The Times *History of the War* states:

*...no action since the first landing did more to cheer the
British forces. It seems to promise further progress. A whole mile
along the coast, five lines of Turkish trenches, about two hundred
prisoners, three mountain guns, and an immense quantity of
small arms ammunition and many rifles were captured during
the operations on 28 June.*

Hamilton in his diary entry for 28 June wrote:

*Hunter Weston, Gouraud and Braithwaite agree that: - had we
only shell to repeat our bombardment of this morning, now, we
could go on another 1000 yards before dark – result Achi Baba
to-morrow or, at the latest, the day after.*

Later on Hamilton wrote that Hunter-Weston and Simpson-Baikie:

*...explain forcibly, not to say explosively, that on the 28th June
the attack would have scored a success equally brilliant to that
achieved by the 29th Division on our left, had we been able to*

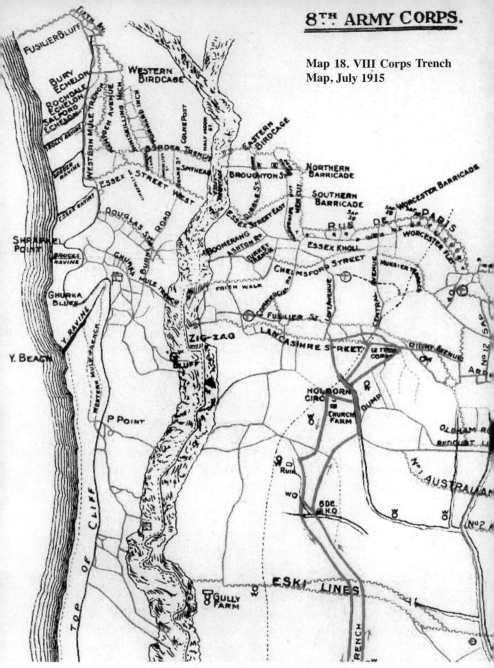

Map 18. VIII Corps Trench Map, July 1915

allot as many a shell to the Turkish trenches assaulted by the 156th Brigade – Lowland Division – as we did to the sector by the sea. But we could not, because, there was not enough stuff in our lockers for the right. Such is war! No use splitting the

difference and trying to win everywhere like high brows halting
between Flanders and Gallipoli. But I am sick at heart, I must
say, to think my brother Scots should have had to catch hold of
the hot end of the poker. Also to think that, with another couple
of hundred rounds, we should have got and held H.12. H.12
which dominates – so prisoners say – the wells whence the
enemy draws water for the whole of his right wing.[5]

If a decision had been made after the failure of the May offensive, in
France, to concentrate all offensive effort at Gallipoli, the success of 28
June might have been made into a strategic victory instead of merely a
brilliant success.

Lance Corporal C. Freestone, 2/South Wales Borderers, was wounded
on 28 June at Gully Ravine, and later on again in the campaign on 21
August 1915. Whilst recovering in the Lily Lane Hospital, Manchester,
he wrote these lines in an autograph book belonging to a Nurse James:

I wanter go back to the trenches
I wanter go back to the Front
I wanter go back to my rifle an' pack
An' hear me old straps creak and grunt
I wanter get back to me blanket
An' sleep on me old little plank
Cos' the cold, clammy sheets that the folks thinks is neat
Makes me shiver like rats in a tank

I wanter get back from the war news
I wanter get back to the hun
I wanter retreat from the chaps in the street
Go' now's or the war should be run
I wanter go back where Tipperary
Ain't whistled from morning till night
I wanter go back where the Zepps don't attack
Cos there ain't any babies to fight

I wanter get back from the flappers
Go rattle their boots an' flags
I wanter vamoose from the bloomin services
An' the wearisome singin of rags
I wanter get back from the motors
An' miners with strikes on the brain
I'm to muddled to think an' I shan't sleep a wink
Till I'm safe back in Gallipoli again.

1. Patterson, J. H., *With the Zionists in Gallipoli*, (1916), p.187.
2. Ryan, D. G. J, *Historical Record of the 6th Gurkha Rifles*, (1925), p.111.
3. Patterson, *Op.Cit.*, (1916), p.188.
4. Ewing, W, Doctor, *From Gallipoli to Baghdad*, (1918), p.90.
5. Hamilton, Sir Ian, *Gallipoli Diary*, (1920), Vol.II, p.9.

Chapter Six

TRENCH WARFARE AT GULLY RAVINE

The successes of the 21 June French attack on the right, and the 28 June British attack on the left at Gully Ravine had given much encouragement to the Allied troops. On 12/13 July another attack was launched in the middle of the line, near Krithia. Casualties were again heavy, and there was only a moderate level of success. The last major action before the evacuation, at Helles, was on 6 August, when diversionary attacks were made to distract the Turks attention from the new landings at Suvla Bay. The Battle of Gully Ravine was the last successful battle in the Helles sector, after which trench warfare set in; trenches were repaired, improved and extended, patrols were sent out and vigilance constantly maintained, all had to be endured under the constant threat from snipers, mining and shellfire.

Life and death went on. On the 2 August whilst in the line at Fusilier Bluff, Lieutenant Melville Hamilton, attached 1/Border Regiment, wrote:

I had one man[1] killed shot through the head by one of our own men from the trench behind, that is the trouble when one is sapping in front of the firing line, especially with new troops, who mostly just shove their rifle up and fire and duck again without taking the least notice in what direction or what objects they are suppose to be aiming at.

RSM John William Graham, 3559, 1/Sussex Yeomanry, hit by a spent bullet on the beach during 19 October 1915, aged forty-six.

He died the same day, and with him we lost a regular soldier of the very finest type of warrant officer and one to whom, since mobilisation, the Regiment had owed a very great deal. He was buried in the Gully and was the first member of the Regiment to give his life for his country.

Graham previously served twenty-one years in the 2/Dragoons (Royal Scots Greys), and 4 years in the Sussex Yeomanry. He was originally buried in Gully Ravine, but after the war his grave could not be positively identified, and he is today commemorated on Special Memorial C. 112 in Twelve Tree Copse Cemetery.

Casualties were a common occurrence every day. This kept the stretcher-bearers and field ambulances, which performed a life saving service in evacuating the wounded from the front, busy in their vital role. Private Richard Yorston, 87/Field Ambulance, worked in Gully Ravine:

> We would go about a mile up the gully and the local unit stretcher-bearers would bring the wounded down to us. They'd been at their local regimental first-aid posts. We had two stretcher places on each side and we'd strap them in. We weren't supposed to carry any others but we'd always take a few if there were any there. We could get about half a dozen on the floor. Once they were loaded on board we got ahead as fast as we could go. We used to take it very softly, very gently. The medical orderly would be on the box and he'd keep an eye on them. The ambulances were square, with canvas tops, an open back and solid rubber tyres. They were driven by four mules with two drivers and the wagon orderly who looked after the patients. I was the wheel driver. It was a bit rough going up, just enough

Ambulance wagon led by horses in the mud – 'The transport was frequently thigh-deep in liquid mud in those evil days.' (IWM Q13648)

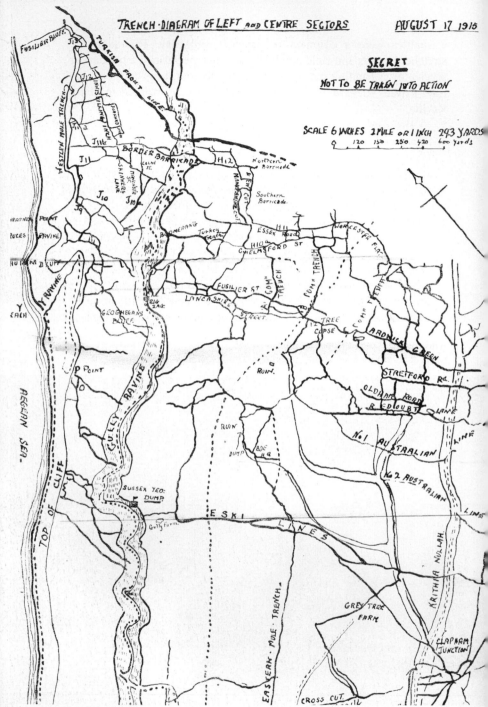

Map 19. VIII Corps Trench Map, August 1915

The 42nd Division (East Lancs) Headquarters in the small gully adjoining Gully Ravine. (WSRC RSR PH 7/11)

> *room for one wagon but you got used to it. We took them right to the dressing station. The nursing orderlies would unload them.*

The 42nd Division took over the Gully Ravine sector from 29th Division in August 1915, settling into their new headquarters on Gully Beach. The bed of the gully then

> *was deep in loose red sand which made very heavy going for tired troops, but when the mud came one sighed for the vanished*

Gully dwellers. (© Chambers)

sand. The transport was frequently thigh-deep in liquid mud in those evil days.

As a rest-bivouac Gully Beach was a great improvement upon all previous resorts, and its attractions read like a holiday advertisement. A sea front, excellent bathing in the Mediterranean, superior accommodation on ledges cut in the cliff face – not unlike a colony of sea-birds – and those who applied early enough even got first-class quarters in a hole in the rock.

460/Battery RFA 'Winter Quarters'. (© Chambers)

In some letters dated September 1915, Noel Sergent, 10/French Artillery, writes of 460/Battery, RFA, which was bivouacked on the coast near Gurkha Bluff:

I went up this ravine for about ten minutes and came to a notice board, 460 Battery Winter Quarters. I asked for Duff and was shown a stairway made of sacks filled with earth leading to the top of the Bluff (Gurkha Bluff). There I found him in his

dugout. He is so situated as to be able to see Imbros and Samothrace and the sea through the ravine; lucky devil! Better than this dust hole! Pat Duff[2] had a touch of fever when I saw him the other day, but he showed me over his battery; his guns seemed very complicated and heavy for field guns. He is beautifully situated with pines and heather and pyrtle and an arbutus bush at the foot of his dugout.[3]

Gully Beach. (IWM Q13649)

A favourite occupation of the troops when off duty was to go fishing off Gully Beach. One popular method employed was to throw pieces of bread into the sea as bait, to be followed with a Mills bomb. The explosion would stun the shoal of fish, which would then be gathered out of the water.
(IWM Q13656)

Executions

Two men were to be executed on Gully Beach, Private Thomas Davis and Sergeant John Robins.

Private Thomas Davis, 1/9804, 1/Royal Munster Fusiliers. Early in the morning of Monday 21 June, Irishman Davis had been posted as a 'flying sentry' to patrol the perimeter of his battalion's headquarters. During a routine check by the duty sergeant it was noticed that Davis was nowhere to be seen. Davis eventually returned to the guardroom about three hours later. Private Davis was thus charged with quitting his post as a sentry, whilst on active service, without permission. He was tried by a Field General Court Martial (FGCM), and sentenced to 'suffer death by being shot'. The excuse of a severe stomach pain making Davis visit the latrine was not believed. Dysentery, or the 'Gallipoli Trot', was at this stage of the campaign becoming renowned throughout the Peninsula. However, this was not the first offence that Davis had committed, having been court-martialled twice since he had landed at Gallipoli. On 5 May 1915, Davis was sentenced to be shot for cowardice, for quitting his post in the face of the enemy. This sentence was later commuted to ten years penal servitude, to be served at the end of the war. Within a week of this promulgation Davis was sentenced to 28 days field punishment number one (being tied to a wagon wheel) for being absent from his piquet. The final sentence was confirmed by Hamilton on 29 June, and at 05:00 on 2 July 1915, whilst the Gully Ravine battle was still raging, Thomas Davis, age twenty-one, was executed on Gully Beach. He has no known grave, and is commemorated on the Helles memorial (Addenda Panel).[4]

Sergeant John Robins, 9610, 5/Wiltshire Regiment, landed in Gallipoli the end of June 1915. Robins, promoted to sergeant during the campaign, refused to accompany an officer on a patrol, as he was unwell. A medical officer prescribed some medicine and Robins was returned to duty. He still maintained that he was too unwell, and refused to accompany the officer on the patrol. On 8 December he was charged with 'wilfully disobeying an order given by a superior officer in the execution of

his duty'. Robins related to the court that during his eight years service in India he had suffered from persistent bouts of fever, which were aggravated by wet weather. Records also showed that twenty-five percent of the battalion were on the sick list at this time. The Field General Court Martial proceedings, verging on being a fiasco[5], were plagued with medical and legal irregularities. Robins was sentenced to death and executed by a party of 8/Cheshire Regiment at 08:05 on 2 January 1916, at a point about 400 yards north of the Gully Ravine mouth. He is commemorated in Twelve Tree Copse Cemetery, as a Private, on special memorial C. 259.

A bullet splattered sniper's plate found on the battlefield. (© Chambers)

British Forward Observation post, near Fusilier Bluff, 1915. Note the snipers shields and trench periscope.

Mining and Gas

A new terror was added to the soldiers' life at Gallipoli towards the end of May 1915. Under Quinn's Post, up at Anzac, the Turks laid and detonated a mine beneath the Australian garrison, wiping out a platoon, and then quickly consolidated the crater into a new position. The mining war had begun, not just at Anzac, but Helles too. During the month of May the Turks, and the British (under the direction of 29th Divisional Engineers) had both exploded mines in the Krithia Nullah area, but it was not until the autumn that mining at Gully Ravine really begun in earnest. Soon a specialised Mining Company was formed under Captain H. W. Laws, Royal Naval Division, which set up its headquarters at Pink Farm. Later given the official title of the VIII Corps Mining Company, it had promising results, although it had few experienced officers and men at its

Tunnellers – An entrance to a mineshaft, near Gully Ravine.

disposal. Extra pay was secured for these men and instruction given on sinking shafts and making galleries by the few experienced miners available. Later, in December 1915, eight officers and eighty-six men of the 254/Tunnelling Company arrived at Gallipoli, to the relief of the veteran tunnellers. Unfortunately this reinforcement was too little, too late as evacuation by then was only weeks away.

The Turks exploded mines on 3, 15, 18, 21, 22 and 29 September, all in the area of the Gridiron, three of which caused some serious damage to the British parapets, one destroying the Birdcage, but this was nothing too serious and could easily be repaired. The British replied with mines on 14, 19 and 22 September. Joseph Murray's book, *Gallipoli As I Saw It*, gives excellent accounts of the mining activity in the Gully Ravine area. On 14 September, Murray (Hood Battalion., RND) had helped lay three ten pound tins of Ammonal. As soon as the men in the front line were warned:

> *...with a terrific bang up went the mine and, with it, the Turkish front line. Our line trembled; huge chunks of earth fell everywhere from the cloud of dust that shrouded the entire scene.*

On 15 September Murray and a colleague were later entombed and made a lucky escape by digging themselves out after the Turks sprang a mine in the same place. The mining game had started.

Mining in this area began as a defensive, but soon became an offensive weapon, with both sides duelling for supremacy. A British tunnel was dug that reached the Gridiron, a Turkish strongpoint on the eastern side of the gully, where a 610-pound mine was laid. On 22 September, shortly before it was fired, the infantry commenced rapid fire as a ruse to bring the Turks into the trenches. The exploding mine completely destroyed the Turkish position, leaving a forty-foot diameter crater behind:

> As our fire lessened, that of the Turks increased and spread to our side of the gully. The sharp crack of the rifles, the rat-a-tat of the machine guns, the deep thud of the shells and the fantastic patterns of the shrapnel bursts above the blue haze were really awesome to us, the onlookers. There was then a tremendous boom, followed by a slowly rising dome of black smoke which seemed reluctant to disperse; for minutes it obscured the whole area...the 610 pounds of Ammonal had done its devastating job.[6]

Later in the day Joseph Murray joined a party of men taking over at No.3 gallery in the same area as the earlier mine:

> We arrived at the appointed time, 6 p.m., and found everything quiet and peaceful and going to plan. No digging had been heard since we left.

After five minutes there were reports of sounds of digging, only about fifteen feet away from the British trench. Then the officer in charge remarked that:

> ...he felt as if he was sitting on top of a volcano waiting for it to erupt. Almost as he spoke that's just what happened. There was a sickening thud; the ground trembled and showers of earth came crashing down upon us, the resultant dust hindering our vision.[7]

The Turks had exploded a large mine, at about 18:00;

> ...the sky was darkened by the earth thrown up, and men in support and reserve trenches were covered with the falling clods[8].

Another crater was formed only just to the left of the British Crater, in No Man's Land. This explosion badly damaged about 300 yards of trench, and destroyed the British mining galleries in the area. Work was at once started to dig a new trench along the back of the crater. As dusk fell Captain Harold Thomas Cawley, 6/Manchester Regiment, a Liberal MP from Prestwich, occupied the newly formed crater with four men, and set about consolidating it by building a barricade. This party stayed in the crater, only 18 yards from the Turkish trenches, exchanging bombs with the Turks all night. The War Diary for the 6/Manchesters goes on to explain that:

> ...the crater was again occupied at dusk, until midnight when there was a suspicion that the Turks were digging towards the crater. CAPT. H. T. CAWLEY firing into the crater to satisfy himself on this front was killed by a bullet through the temple. He is an irreplaceable loss to the Battn.[9]

Captain Cawley was buried at 15:00 the following day at Lancashire Landing Cemetery, in the presence of Major-General Douglas, Brigadier-General Elliot and his commanding officer. In his honour the crater was named Cawley's Crater.

Captain Harold Thomas Cawley, 6/Manchesters, was one of four sons of Sir Frederick Cawley, Chancellor of the Duchy of Lancaster. Two of his brothers, John and Oswald, were also to die in the Great War. Cawley was ADC to Major-General W. Douglas CB DSO, landing at Gallipoli in May 1915. At the beginning of September he was given permission, at his request, to return to his battalion, leaving the comparative safety of Divisional HQ. He wrote in a letter,

> I told the General I wanted to join the Battn; and he has sent the application forward: I was ashamed of being behind here whilst all those fellows were being killed.

From *The House of Commons Book of Remembrance, 1914-18*, page 16:

> Captain Cawley was a very brave and unassuming gentleman; one of his exploits is worth recounting. A small ammunition cart had been taken up the principal nullah, which the men proceeded to unload in order to carry the cases to the dugout. The enemy spotted this wagon and immediately started to shell it vigorously with shrapnel. Naturally there was a slight hesitancy on the part of the men unloading as to what was the wisest thing to do. Captain Cawley settled the situation by getting off his horse into the cart and handing the boxes down double-quick. After the vehicle was clear, he coolly rode away.

In the October 27, 1915, issue

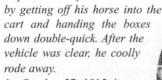

GULLY RAVINE   BORDER BARRICADE   CAWLEY'S CRATER   BIRDCAGE   FUSILIER BLUFF

Site of Cawleys Crater and the Eastern Birdcage. (© Chambers)

of *The Bury Times*, a letter from an unnamed officer is quoted:

You will have seen a notice of poor Cawley's death in the papers. By a strange accident I was talking to him the day before, I had not seen him for years. The 6th Manchesters, his regiment, were holding the line we were going to hold, and I went up the day before to have a look at it. Cawley was commanding a section of the line where a night or two before the enemy had exploded a mine, making a huge crater, on one side of which our new firing line was established, the Turks being on the other and only a little distance away. Cawley was showing me this and the disposition of his bombers, for the place was one to be held most effectively by a bombing party. When we were marching up the next day I heard he had been killed. It appears that the same night, in order to reconnoitre, he crawled up the far side of the crater, and as the moon was bright and the Turkish line only a few yards away, he was at once shot through the head and killed. He was a nice fellow, and his spirit is shown by the fact of his throwing up a soft job on the staff in order to take on ordinary regiment duties in the firing line. He was a member of the Kersal Football Club when I was, about 1899. Cawley was killed in the early morning of Friday 24th ult., and we moved into the line the same day. As we marched up I came across his body lying on a stretcher waiting to go down for burial...

On 13 October the Turks sprang another mine, probably a camouflet,[10] near Cawley's Crater that temporary buried three British men in a tunnel. On 29 October, another Turkish mine was blown that formed a crater by Cawley's Crater. This one destroyed fifteen yards of trench, killing two men, and burying six others. Of the six, three were soon dug out. The other three were miners who were working beneath the

A contemporary sketch of Union Street, near the Birdcage.

GALLIPOLI PENINSULA
— SOUTHERN ZONE —

MAP SHEWING BRITISH TRENCHES AND TURKISH FRONT LINE

SCALE

AEGEAN SEA

Map 20. Trench Map
showing the Turkish
defences north of Gully
Ravine, October 1915.

REFERENCE:—
Traversed Trenches
Main & Communication Trenches
Footpaths "
Roads
Dressing Stations
Wells

crater on the face of a new tunnel. They could not be found and efforts to extract them were soon given up. Amazingly three days later all three managed to get out. Two were carried away on stretchers (Private P. Dennis and another man whose name is not known), but Private J. Grimes of the 5/Manchester Regiment, even though on the point of collapsing, refused to be carried, walking out unaided. All three had had no food for three days and only one bottle of water to share. It was largely due to the determination of Private Grimes that they had dug themselves out, using one pocket-knife, through twelve feet of earth to safety. They received a congratulatory message from G.O.C VIII Corps on their safe return.

The British soon gained the upper hand in mining, and generally all was fairly quiet from this point on. The

On 29 November Second Lieutenant Vincent McNamara, 136/Fortress Company, Royal Engineers, was killed, aged twenty-four years, in a tunnel. He had studied engineering at Cork University and played in six international football matches. A mine was exploded under the Turks, and McNamara went down to inspect the gallery. He collapsed as a result of gas caused by the explosion. After desperate rescue attempts, he was finally removed from the tunnel, but artificial respiration failed, McNamara dying of asphyxiation. He is buried at Lancashire Landing Cemetery. (© Chambers)

A large tunnel/dugout in Gully Ravine. (© Chambers)

Border Barricade in October 1915.

ground around Gully Ravine, at the Gridiron and Fusilier Bluff, was ideal as it consisted mainly of sandstone, so was easily mined for the first fifteen feet. Occasionally the ground proved very hard, and boulders were frequently met with, so that extensive blasting was necessary. By the end of October however, due to the intense mining that had already honeycombed these areas, deeper systems had to be dug. At Fusilier Bluff, three tunnels were actually dug from the cliff face, at a depth of forty feet, towards the Turkish lines. Some of these galleries later formed a type of underground redoubt, even with loopholes for the infantry to fire out of.

On 25 November the Turks broke into a British tunnel near Fusilier Bluff, where they

> *injected through a hole in one of the galleries an aromatic gas, which affected the eyes, but not the lungs.*[11]

This was probably a type of lachrymatory gas and thus not very strong. The hole was quickly sealed and a fire built to help clear out the gas. There is no confirmed record of poisonous gas ever being used at Gallipoli, but as a precautionary measure, during June 1915, 'Hypo' helmet gas masks started to be issued to the troops in order to meet any risk of a gas attack. The horrors of this form of warfare had been seen on the Western Front for the first time in April 1915, when the Germans first used gas at Ypres. Later on in 1915 the troops were instructed to carry two gas helmets, a Hypo helmet to be housed in a home made pocket inside the tunic, and a 'P' (Phenate) Helmet to be carried in a bag over the shoulder.

Map 21. Trench Map indicating the mining activity in the area

Whilst in the line at Border Barricade, Lieutenant Melville Hamilton, attached 1/Border Regiment, wrote in a letter home, dated 26 July 1915:

> We have all now been issued with gas helmets which are much better than the old respirators and also much easier to adjust, not that I think there is much chance of the Turks ever using gas, unless it is in shells, as there is nearly always too much wind for it on the Peninsula.

British Intelligence were aware that German chemical warfare experts had arrived in Constantinople, but gas was never added to the horrors already experienced by the men on Gallipoli. The threat of this method of warfare did however cause some considerable concern. In the 1/Sussex Yeomanry history it was recalled that on one morning a mist or vapour floated towards the trenches of 'C' Squadron, and rolled down into the trench. A couple of men were affected, but it was never ascertained what this mystery vapour was. If it was poisonous gas, it had little effect and was never repeated. On 9 October, at Suvla, the Royal Munster Fusiliers reported their first experience of being gassed, when tear-gas was used on them. This affected some of the men, but luckily it was not a more deadly gas as only half the men had gas respirators issued. The British High Command had other ideas, and planned to add poisonous gas to its Gallipoli arsenal. In November 1915, Captain Garden and twelve gas corporals embarked for Alexandria, Egypt, with 6,000 gas-filled cylinders, to be used at Gallipoli. However, the British command on the Peninsula refused to initiate chemical warfare, as conditions were bad enough already. Moreover, the evacuation was soon to take place. On the Peninsula it was not only unpredictably breezy, but also the Turks had most of the upper ground, so gas would have been of little use. During the gas unit's voyage to Egypt there was almost a mutiny as some cylinders began to leak. This caused great and understandable panic amongst the ship's crew. The party soon returned to France, their mission unaccomplished.

On 19 December a diversion was created at Helles in order to attract Turkish attention away from the evacuation that was taking place at Suvla and Anzac. In a grand finale, more than twenty small British mines were exploded, followed by an infantry attack. Although to a degree only a demonstration, it did show what could be achieved with mine warfare. A watching staff officer exclaimed, 'why on earth didn't we think of this before?'[12] In June 1917, the Messines Ridge, south of Ypres, was to be torn open by a similar 'demonstration' that allowed its successful capture by the British.

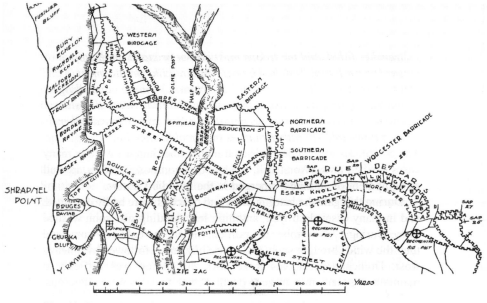

Map 22. Trench Map of the northern part of Gully Ravine

The Winter

The beginning of November brought occasional heavy showers and frost as winter moved in. Between 15 and 17 November the weather took a turn for the worse when a violent storm broke out, along with torrential rain. This turned the ravine into a temporary lake, dammed by huge piles of debris that were soon washed down through the ravine to the sea. The trenches above were initially flooded out, with equipment, rifles and clothing either being soaked through or buried in the mud. The water soon drained off either to the sea or, worse, into the gully. Those with bivouacs on the beach had them washed away by the heavy seas that battered the shoreline all along the coast, making the beach road impassable. Those encamped in the ravine met a similar fate from the torrential waters rushing through:

> Gully Ravine degenerated into an evil-smelling bog; conditions near the front lines were not dissimilar to those experienced in Flanders, with carts bogged down to their axles, trench floors awash with slimy, glutinous mud, and horses struggling through the mire.[13]

On the night of 26 November an even fiercer storm hit the Peninsula:

> ...a storm as disastrous to the combatants as any that ever affected armies in the field. The flood-gates of heaven indeed opened and at Anzac and Suvla the trenches were quickly waist deep, and the current swept down like a mill-race – kit, equipment, rations, even men, being washed away. In places the

143

the coming blast. Immediately he threw himself down onto the bomb, the blast killing him instantly. Two others were slightly wounded. His *London Gazette* citation reads

> *For most conspicuous bravery. He was in the act of throwing a bomb when it slipped from his hand and fell to the bottom of the trench, close to several of our officers and men. He immediately shouted a warning, and himself jumped clear into safety; but, seeing that the officers and men were unable to get into cover, and knowing well that the bomb was due to explode, he returned without hesitation and flung himself on it. He was instantly killed by the explosion. His magnificent act of self sacrifice undoubtedly saved many lives.*

He was buried at the head of Y ravine with the inscription: 'he gave his life to save others'. Today his grave is relocated in Twelve Tree Copse Cemetery with the epitaph 'sunset and evening star and one clear call for me'. His act of self-sacrifice epitomises much of the bravery throughout the Gallipoli campaign where, in many poorly planned attacks, men without question or hesitation sacrificed their lives.

Every night ships were coming into Gully Beach, and the other beaches further south, to take off the weary troops. Each evening the Helles stronghold slowly dwindled, disappearing into the night. At midday, 7 January, one day before the final evacuation, the Turks began a heavy bombardment at Fusilier Bluff, and at 16:00 two Turkish mines were exploded, one opposite Fusilier Bluff and the other at the Birdcage. These were the last two mines ever fired at Gallipoli. The diary entry for this day by Captain R. C. W. Burn, 1/Sussex Yeomanry Machine Gun Officer, said:

> *I watched the bombardment, which looked horrible; the whole place a mass of bursting shells; and hidden from view by black and yellow smoke with the white puff of shrapnel incessantly coming through the lot. Of course most of our guns have gone – which has made it worse; and it was pitiful to hear the solitary guns replying to this wall of high explosive; the parapets were badly damaged; but all is well and the night passed quietly.*

The Turks (12th Division) then attacked en masse, but were driven off by the 7/North Staffordshire Regiment[15], part of the skeleton force left to defend the line, with the help of the Navy and the few artillery pieces left. The Turkish attack lacked any great vigour, leaving their trenches in two positions only, and was probably just a probing action to see whether the British were still there. The earlier Turkish bombardment had taken its toll; fifty-eight were killed in this attack, including the North Staffs' Commanding Officer, Lieutenant-Colonel Francis

146

'A serious accident occurred' – the beached K lighter and Gully Pier in 1919

The same scene today. (© Chambers)

Hercules Walker[16]. These were the last British troops killed at Helles in an action. By 18:00 that afternoon the attack was over.

During the final phase of the evacuation, at 02:20 hours on 9 January 1916, 'a serious accident occurred' when a lighter ran aground at Gully Beach, and could not be re-floated. This lighter was one of two provided by HMS *Talbot* to take the last few men off Gully Beach, but it was driven aground by the heavy Aegean seas that were sweeping over Gully pier. The first lighter set off successfully with about 500 men, but the second became firmly beached. The remaining troops, about 160 men, including Major-General Sir Stanley Maude, had to disembark and march down to W Beach.

Private Sid Blythman, 5/Wiltshire Regiment, was part of the rearguard who recalls the incident:

> *Myself and my pal Cheshire and an officer had a post and the barbed wire gap across Y Gully, which all the troops in that sector had to pass through. Our officers checked them all, and then two Royal Engineers closed the barbed wire gap and we made our way down the gully to the beach, only to be told the boat that was to take us off had run aground and we were to proceed along the*

coast to W Beach. I think there were about 60 of us who had all been on different jobs and we had two miles to go. With no one in the trenches it was a bit of a nervy experience – thank goodness the Navy kept up a bombardment. Anyhow, we made it to W Beach and got away on the last lighter and were taken to Imbros.[17]

The men reached W Beach at about 03:25, but Maude was nowhere to be seen. He had left his valise on the stranded lighter, so had set off back to Gully Beach with his chief of staff to recover it. He finally arrived back at W Beach, twenty minutes later, carrying his valise on a wheeled stretcher, just moments before the last boats were about to leave. Leaving a general behind would have taken some explaining.

An original song called '*Come Into the Garden, Maude*', composed by Michael W. Balfe, from the original poem by Tennyson, was parodied at concert parties after the evacuation:

Come into the lighter, Maude,
The fuse has long been lit,
Come into the lighter, Maude,
And never mind your kit.
The waves grow high,
But what care I,
I'd rather be seasick,
Than blown sky-high.
So, come into the lighter Maude,
Or I'm off in the launch alone!

1. Believed to be Private James Whitworth, 19076, aged 22 from 'B' Company, 1/Border Regiment. He is buried in Twelve Tree Copse cemetery.
2. Sir Patrick Duff later had a distinguished career as Principle Private Secretary to Prime Minister Stanley Baldwin, and was later Deputy High Commissioner in Canada and High Commissioner in New Zealand.
3. 'With The French Artillery' by J.N.B Sergeant, *The Gallipolian*, No.67, Christmas 1991, p.21.
4. One other British soldier was executed at Gallipoli, Private Harry Salter, 6/East Lancashire Regiment, at Suvla on 11 December 1915 for desertion.
5. Putkowski, Julian and Sykes, Julian, *Shot at Dawn*, (1989), pp.61-62.
6. Murray, Joseph, *Gallipoli As I Saw It*, (1965), p.125.
7. Ibid., p.126.
8. Gibbon, Frederick P., *The 42nd (East Lancashire) Division 1914-1918*, (1920), p.53.
9. PRO WO95/4316 War Diary, 6/Manchester Regiment
10. A camouflet was a small mine that was extensively used in counter-mining. The force of the explosion was expended underground, and rarely brokes the surface.
11. Gibbon, *Op.Cit.*, (1920), p.54.
12. Grieve, *Op.Cit.*, (1936), p.86.
13. Rhodes James, Robert, Gallipoli, (1965), p.343.
14. Gibbon, Op.Cit., (1920), p.55.
15. 13th Division was holding Gully Spur at this time.
16. Lieutenant-Colonel Francis Hercules Walker, aged 46, is commemorated on the Helles memorial (Panel 170-171).
17. Letter from Sid Blythman on the evacuation, *The Gallipolian*, No.51, Summer 1986, p.19.

Chapter Seven

GULLY RAVINE TODAY

Equipment: When visiting the battlefields, preferably with at least one other person, take a good supply of bottled water, a walking stick (also useful to fend off any farm dogs), sun cream, hat, long trousers, camera/binoculars, pen/notepad, penknife and sturdy boots with ankle support. If you are unfamiliar with the area, and going off the beaten track, a map and compass is recommended. Put this altogether in a small rucksack with a first aid kit and this book, and you should have a good recipe for an informative trip. A mobile phone can also be useful in emergencies (with the number of hotel, local emergency services and the car-hire company). It is also a good idea to tell someone else where you are planning to go for the day, and what time you are planning to return. Most importantly, bring a good supply of film (100, 200 or 400 ASA). The Holt's guide and map, along with the Cupper/Taylor book is also useful to have with you.

Warning: Do not forget that the whole of the Gallipoli Peninsula is a national historical 'Peace Park', dedicated to the memory of those who died on both sides. Please respect this. A lot of the area is still farmland and private property. When walking please be aware of the crops and respect the privacy of the people who live here. If you do find a wartime relic, like a shell, grenade or bullet, please leave it alone. Photograph it by all means, but please do not touch it as these things are usually in a highly dangerous condition, and can still cause death and injury. It is strictly forbidden by the Turkish authorities to remove any artefact from the battlefield.

Always visit Gully Ravine in summer, never in winter when the rain can turn the gentle gully stream into a torrential river. Even in the dry season the stream can still trickle, and in places mud can be quite deep, so be very careful. Also beware of the remains of overgrown trenches and shell holes that are covered in thick prickly scrub. The overgrowth disguises many small holes and rocks that can easily send one falling. A sprained ankle is the last thing you want in this remote region. Occasionally you may meet a dog from one of the local farms or goatherd. Take along a stick, and try and stay well clear of any goats. The dogs are just protecting their herd and territory, and in my experience their bark is worst than their bite.

Remember that once inside Gully Ravine you are in one of the most isolated places on the Peninsula, a long way from any house and any populated area of any kind...you are on your own, so take all necessary precautions.

The gully in places can stretch anywhere from a couple of metres, to almost forty metres wide, with the dried-up streambed forming the pathway, meandering along the gully floor. Dotted throughout with wild grasses and small bushes, the sandy gully floor is near-enough flat, with only a slight incline that is not noticeable, so the walking is not too strenuous. The ridges and walls of the ravine are thickly populated with pine trees, interspersed in places with long grasses and scrub. The only place where nothing grows is where the ravine walls are too steep to support the vegetation, leaving the wall sun-scorched and barren.

Under the terms of the Armistice with Turkey the British Army re-entered the Peninsula at the end of 1918 and cleared the battlefields of the bodies still unburied. You will find that the Commonwealth War Graves Commission cemeteries at Gallipoli are different to those in Belgium or France. Because of the nature of the ground they have small tilted sandstone tablets for grave headstones. The Stone of Remembrance and white stone Cross of Sacrifice, a slightly different style than those found in Europe, can also be found in all the cemeteries. Row after row of headstones are interspersed with small plants and shrubs that adorn many of the beautifully kept cemeteries. Mature trees, including the odd Judas Tree (Cercis siliquastrum: the tree that Judas was believed to have hung himself from in his remorse at having betrayed Jesus), grow majestically, providing valuable shade on a hot sunny day:

> *Beside the ruins of Troy they lie buried, those men so beautiful; there they have their burial-place, hidden in an enemy's land.*

The Agamemnon, 453-455

Chapter Eight

Tour 1: Gully Ravine battlefield by car

This tour, taking about three hours, takes you around the Gully Ravine battlefield without the need for lengthy walks. Even if you are planning to do the walks, I recommend doing this tour first, as it will give an excellent overview of the area, allowing you to orientate yourselves.

Begin at the Helles Memorial.

Helles Memorial to the Missing

Designed by Sir John Burnet, the Helles Memorial was completed in the summer of 1924, and:

> ...is a symbol of triumph – the triumph of human nature over fearful odds; a great nation's willing sacrifice for an idea. Having suffered this splendid failure, Britain has had the courage to ignore the defeat and commemorate in stone those who never questioned the worth or wisdom of the idea. The sacrifice and valour were things far greater than the un-acquired victory. [1]

The memorial contains 20,763 names of men who fell in the Gallipoli campaign whose graves are unknown or who were lost or buried at sea. The memorial stands on the tip of the Peninsula in a form of an obelisk, over thirty metres high, on top of a hill. This hill was known to the British as Guezji Baba, and to the Turks as Göztepe (Eye Hill). A redoubt originally stood on this ground that helped bar the way, along with Hill 138 (Hunter Weston Hill), between the forces on W and V beaches on 25 April 1915, until captured by 4/Worcestershire Regiment later that day.

Helles Memorial with the Krupp gun positions. (© Chambers)

The view, looking north, from Hunter-Weston Hill (Hill 138). (© Chambers)

Among those commemorated on the Helles Memorial who have a connection with Gully Ravine, are the **Murdoch** (Panels 92-97) and **Thomson** brothers (Panels 26-30), killed during the Battle of Gully Ravine, whilst assaulting H.12, on 28 June 1915. **Private Gavin Murdoch, Private Ronald Murdoch** and **Private William Murdoch,** 8/Cameronians (Scottish Rifles), and **Lieutenant Eric James Thomson** and **Second Lieutenant Francis Wishart Thomson**, 7/Royal Scots (Leith) Battalion. Also listed are **Lieutenant-Colonel Walker,** 7/North Staffs (Panel 170-171) who was killed in the last major action at Gully Ravine on 7 January 1916. **T/Major Cuthbert Bromley VC** (Panel 218) and **Captain Gerald Robert O'Sullivan VC** (Panel 97) are also commemorated on the memorial.

It is worth spending a little time at the Helles Memorial as you are at a good vantage point for viewing the battlefield, from S Beach and the Turkish Memorial to the east, over to W Beach down on the West. Achi Baba sits in the middle, with the village of Krithia on its western spur with Gully Ravine winding its way north through the fir tree line on the western side.

In the immediate fields near the memorial are two Krupp guns dated 1898. The first is situated in a shallow, scrub filled hollow about twenty metres north of the memorial wall, and the second is about thirty metres south, in a hollow between the memorial and lighthouse. When there are no crops they are fairly easy to locate. From the Helles Memorial proceed towards Lancashire Landing Cemetery, passing Hunter Weston Hill.

Lancashire Landing Cemetery

The cemetery, started immediately after the April landings, stands on a small ridge named Karaja Oghul Tepe that leads up to Hill 114 (Tekke Burnu). There are a total of 1,171 graves from the United Kingdom, twenty-seven from Australia, fifteen from New Zealand, two from Canada, one man from the Zion Mule Corps, another from the local Mule Corps and seventeen Greek labourers. The unidentified graves number 135, with eleven special memorials to those who are known to be buried here. There are also graves moved here after the war from the islands of Imbros and Tenedos. The register contains details of 1,101 burials and commemorations.

Among those buried in the cemetery are **Captain Cawley MP** (row A, grave 76), killed defending a mine crater (Cawley's Crater), **Lieutenant McNamara** (row L, grave 9), a tunnelling officer who was asphyxiated in a mine gallery near the ravine, and **Lance-Sergeant Keneally VC** (row C, grave 104) who won his

Victoria Cross during the W Beach (Lancashire) landings, to die of wounds received at the Gully Ravine battle on 29 June 1915. Note that his name is incorrectly spelt on the headstone.

Leaving the cemetery, follow the road west for 400 metres; passing the old ruins of the post-war Turkish Army camp on the left (if you turn off at the old camp, a track will take you down onto W Beach). Where the road comes to a northerly bend, down below is Bakery Beach, site of a wartime bakery that first produced fresh bread on 21 May 1915. Joseph Murray visited Bakery Beach on 19 November 1915, and wrote:

> I followed the Aegean coast by way of a track skirting Hill 114 and then down the cliffs again to Bakery Beach. I had not been here before or even known of its existence but it was not much of a place.[2]

Continue along the road and after half a kilometre you will see a small track leading down onto X Beach. This is where 2/Royal Fusiliers landed on 25 April. Continuing on you soon come to a right hand bend. To the left are Gully Beach and the beginning of Gully Ravine, masked from view by pine trees. Park under the shelter of the trees on the eastern side of the road and follow the rough track down onto Gully Beach. See *Tour 2: Gully Ravine and Beach*, for details on the area, including the Beach, Pier, Lighter, Well and Gully Ridge. Return to your vehicle and continue along the road to Pink Farm Cemetery, approximately half a kilometre further along the road.

Pink Farm Cemetery

In 1915 Pink Farm was a ruined stone building close to a cart track, called West Krithia Road, set in a pretty countryside location. The war was soon to change this. In a letter from Noel Sergent, who served in 10/French Artillery, he writes that after he left Pink Farm, he:

> ...came into the loveliest country. I could hardly believe my eyes; it was just like Valescure. Small tufts of pine trees, thyme, donkey-pepper and heather.[3]

Today, little has changed, nature reclaiming its beauty from its worn-torn past.

Pink Farm Cemetery is actually situated about fifty metres southwest of the original Pink Farm, on the old track to the once neighbouring Grey Tree Farm. The present day road outside the cemetery follows the old path of the West Krithia Road, parallel to the coast. Originally called Sotiri Farm by the locals, it was known to the troops as Pink Farm because of the colour of the soil in the area. During the campaign Pink Farm was used as a forward supply dump,

Pink Farm Cemetery. (© Chambers)

and served as the headquarters for the VIII Corps Mining Company. The farm also acted as a collection point for the wounded from the front line; from here on they were taken to the field hospitals by mule-drawn ambulance or stretcher-bearer if needed. The foundations of the farm along with its well and old water pump can still be seen today. In the surrounding woods there are also remains of trenches and dugouts.

The grave concentration at Pink Farm Cemetery, begun in late April 1915, contains several smaller cemeteries that were collected together after the armistice. During the campaign there were originally three cemeteries here, Pink Farm No.1, No.2 and No.3. After the war these and six other smaller cemeteries, being 29th Division Cemetery, 52nd Division Cemetery, Aerodrome Cemetery, Oak Tree Cemetery, Gully Beach Cemetery and Gully Farm Cemetery were all brought together.

Pink Farm Cemetery contains a total of 602 graves: 209 United Kingdom forces, three from New Zealand, two from Australia, five Indian Army and 164 unidentified. The unnamed graves number 250. The total number of burials in the cemetery is 383 and special memorial tablets amount to 219. The register contains details of 352 burials and commemorations. It is interesting to note that most of the unidentified graves are on the higher level, and the identified on the lower level.

Amongst those buried here are **Captain C. W. Birdwood**, 6/Gurkhas, who was mortally wounded during the 4 June attack on Mushroom Redoubt. He died of wounds on 7 June at the 108/Indian Field Ambulance on Gully Beach, aged 33 (plot IV, row A, grave 6). Privates **Frank Baden** (Special Memorial 121) and **Frank Gough** (Special Memorial 148) are also buried here. They were accidentally killed during the night of 18/19 July by falling rocks, so be careful near the cliff and ravine edges.

Grave of Private F. Baden, accidentally killed by falling rocks. (© Chambers)

Continue along the road from Pink Farm towards Alçitepe (Krithia). After about 400 metres there is a rough track leading towards the gully on the western side of the road. See *Tour 3: Gully Ravine and Pink Farm,* if you would like a walk in and around the Gully Ravine area at this point. Continue along the road, and after another one and a half kilometres you will pass over the site of the Eski lines. Continue along the road for another kilometre, passing Fir Tree Wood and the Daisy Patch, before arriving at Twelve Tree Copse Cemetery.

Twelve Tree Copse Cemetery

Twelve Tree Copse was originally a small group of pine trees, situated just south of the present day cemetery, named by the men of the 29th Division when they reached this area on 28 April 1915. During the Battle of Gully Ravine this copse was used as a forward observation post, but later on in the

Twelve Tree Copse Cemetery, with its distinctive trees. (© Chambers)

campaign shellfire destroyed all the trees. Replacement pine trees have now been planted in the cemetery in recognition of the original name. The copse is set a few yards north of Fir Tree Wood, by the pre-war West Krithia Road that went north from W Beach, through Pink Farm and eventually entering the village of Krithia. The modern day road follows this very closely.

Twelve Tree Copse Cemetery contains a total of 3360 graves. It is about 800 metres southwest of the village of Alçitepe (Krithia). During the war there was no cemetery at Twelve Tree Copse; it was formed after the Armistice by the concentration of smaller cemeteries and isolated graves from the battlefield of April to August and December 1915. It covers an area of 9,307 square yards, and contains the graves of 462 soldiers from the United Kingdom, thirteen from New Zealand, two from Australia, and 1,953 whose units could not be ascertained. The unnamed graves number 2,226; and special memorials are erected to 644 soldiers from the United Kingdom, ten from New Zealand, one from Australia, and two from India are known or believed to be buried among them. There is also a New Zealand Memorial, one of four on the Peninsula, with names of those killed in the Second Battle of Krithia, May 1915.

Of the special tablets, forty-seven are to 7/Cameronians (Scottish Rifles) who fell on the 28 June, and a lot of the unknown are probably also from this date or the Suvla diversionary actions at Helles on 6 August 1915. There are also 142 burials from the 1/Essex Regiment who fell during 6 August. The Register records particulars of 2,703 burials.

The cemetery rises to the northwest in three terraces and can be seen from the main inland Alçitepe road, looking west from Redoubt Cemetery. The most important burial ground concentrated into Twelve Tree Copse Cemetery was Geoghegan's Bluff Cemetery, originally located near the Zig-Zag at Gully Ravine, that contained the graves of 925 men, many of these fallen in the June Gully Ravine fighting. Others include Fir Tree Wood Cemetery, originally located slightly south of Twelve Tree Copse, which contained a lot of graves from the May fighting, in particular from the 29th Division and also the New Zealand Brigade. The third is Clunes Vennel Cemetery, which was located just south of Krithia where 522 soldiers were buried. All these cemeteries had their bodies exhumed by the Graves Registration Unit in 1919.

Three senior officers of 156 Brigade are buried here, **Brigadier-General William Scott-Moncrieff**, Officer Commanding 156 Brigade, (Special

Memorial C. 132), **Lieutenant Colonel John Boyd Wilson**, CO 7/Cameronians (Special Memorial C. 406) and **Lieutenant Colonel Henry Hannan**, CO 8/Cameronians (plot VII, row A, grave 7), who was shot by a sniper whilst watching the French attack on 21 June 1915.

Others buried here include **Second Lieutenant Alfred Smith VC**, *Croix de Guerre*, age twenty-four, 5/East Lancashire Regiment, who posthumously won his Victoria Cross at Fusilier Bluff. He was originally buried in a battlefield grave above Y Beach, but his body was exhumed after the war (Special Memorial C. 358). **Sergeant John Robins**, 9610, 5/Wiltshire Regiment, was one of three Gallipoli men executed during the campaign. Robins was 'shot at dawn' at 08:05 at Gully Beach on 2 January 1916 charged with 'wilfully disobeying an order given by a superior officer in the execution of his duty'. He is commemorated on Special Memorial C. 259 as a private. **RSM John William Graham**, 3559, 1/Sussex Yeomanry, hit by a spent bullet in the rest area on 19 October 1915, aged forty-six (Special Memorial C. 112). **Major James Norman Henderson**, aged thirty-four, 4/Royal Scots, was killed in action on 28 June 1915. He had both legs smashed during the Turkish counter bombardment before the attack. Whilst he was being attended to in a dugout in a support trench, another shell burst killing him and all inside. (Special Memorial C. 330). **Captain Harold Robert Clayton**, 1/Lancashire Fusiliers, a Boer War veteran, was killed on 4 June 1915. His body lay visible, hanging from the Turkish wire until two months later, when members of the King's Own Scottish Borderers recovered his remains for burial on 6 August 1915. After the war the Graves Registration unit could not positively identify his grave. His epitaph on his gravestone reads: DEAR OLD HAROLD. (Special Memorial B. 8). **Captain Hugh Richard Augustin Whytehead**, 6/Gurkhas, was killed in the attack on KOSB Trench on 22 May 1915, aged thirty-four. He was buried next day immediately above Y Beach on the southwest side of Gurkha Ravine. His grave was moved from this site to Twelve Tree Copse after the war. (Special Memorial C. 456). **Lieutenant Lawrence Clive Boustead**, 1/Royal Dublin Fusiliers, was killed in action on 28 June 1915, aged twenty-one. He was originally buried in Geoghegan's Bluff; but after the war his remains were moved to a grave (plot VII, row B, grave 3) in the Geoghegan's Bluff Plot at Twelve Tree Copse. **Petty Officer Mechanic R. R. Thomas**, F/1693, 4/Squadron Royal Naval Armoured Car Division, RNAS, is buried here, killed at his Maxim gun whilst supporting the 28 June attack (plot VII, row C, grave 18).

Leaving Twelve Tree Copse Cemetery you will very soon reach the village

The village of Krithia today. Note the sign to Nuri Yamut (Fusilier Bluff). (© Chambers)

Entrance to the Krithia Military Museum.
(© Chambers)

of Alçitepe (Krithia), about a kilometre further north. When you reach Alçitepe a visit to the privately owned Military Museum is recommended. This contains many battlefield artefacts, photographs, letters etc. There is no entrance fee, but voluntary contributions in the donations box help with the upkeep. Refreshments can also be purchased here or in the village (two other museums worth visiting are the Turkish Canakkale Martyrs' Memorial and the War Relics Museum at Morto Bay and the Gaba Tepe Information Centre and Museum at Anzac). The British never captured Krithia, objective for 25 April. Ottoman Greeks were settled in the village before the war, but were later moved to Anatolia during the military build up on the Peninsula in 1915. To the east of the village there used to be a small cluster of windmills, used for extracting oil from olives, but all of these were destroyed during the war. The Ottoman Turks knew the village as Kirte then, but when it was resettled in the 1930s it was renamed Alçitepe.

Leave Alçitepe; take the road that veers off in a westerly direction, towards Fusilier Bluff, sign posted to Nuri Yamut. After about half a kilometre you will soon reach the Son Ok Memorial.

Son Ok ('Last Arrow') Turkish Memorial

The obelisk type memorial was built in 1948 by the Turkish Government to commemorate an action during the Third Battle of Krithia. The inscription translates:

> The gunners of a 12 cm siege battery defeated the enemy at this point by a bayonet charge and so secured the Third Victory of Kirte, 7 June 1915.

Continue along the road for another half a kilometre, noting that the road dips down into the northern end of Gully Ravine and the Nullah. Situated at the top end of the ravine is a statue of a Turkish Soldier.

Son Ok Memorial.
(© Chambers)

Turkish Soldier Statue at the top end of Gully Ravine. (© Chambers)

Turkish Soldier Statue

This memorial was erected in the 1990s. Note that the Turkish soldier appears to be holding a British No.4 SMLE, a weapon that only began to be issued during the Second World War. Although inaccurate in detail, this is still an awe inspiring statue, facing towards the direction of the British advance.

Follow the road a few metres further, deeper down into the ravine, where you will arrive at the Zigindere Field Dressing Station Memorial and Cemetery.

Zigindere Field Dressing Station Turkish Cemetery and Memorials

Situated at the top end of Zigindere (Gully Ravine), the memorial and cemetery were built in 1943, and recently renovated in 1992. This is the original site of a Turkish dressing station that acted as a forward First Aid Post for treating and evacuating the wounded. Because of its close proximity to the front, it was heavily shelled, especially during the actions fought here. On the bridge that crosses the Zigin stream there are two memorial tablets to record the British shelling of this dressing station, which resulted in many Turkish wounded being killed. During one such shelling Captain Kemal Bey, Staff Commander of the 2nd Turkish Division, was killed, and is commemorated by the sculpture of the wounded Turkish soldiers. This sculpture also commemorates the wounded of the 25 and 26/Infantry Regiments (9th Turkish Division). It is of interest to note that the cemetery is more symbolic than being an actual marked burial ground. Many of the other Turkish cemeteries on the Peninsula are also symbolic, although this one most probably contains burials.

From here continue up out of the ravine where the road soon ends at Fusilier Bluff with the Turkish Nuri Yamut Memorial.

Turkish Ziindere Field Dressing Station Memorial and Cemetery. (© Chambers)

Nuri Yamut Turkish Cemetery and Memorial

Overlooking Fusilier Bluff, and situated between Fifth Avenue and the old Turkish front line, is the pinkish coloured Nuri Yamut Memorial (Sargiyeri Sehitligi) that commemorates the 10,000 Turkish soldiers that were killed on the Zigindere Front from 26 June to 12 July 1915 (Battle of Gully Ravine). Lieutenant-General Nuri Yamut, who was the commanding officer of the Gelibolu II Corps, erected this memorial after the war. It reads SEHIDLIK 1915 (To the Martyrs who died in the Battle, 1915). The walled area around the memorial contains graves of Turkish dead. It was in this northernmost area of the battlefield that Second-Lieutenant Alfred Smith won his Victoria Cross.

See *Tour 5: Fusilier Bluff to Y Beach*, if you would like a walk in and around the Gully Ravine area at this point.

Nuri Yamut Memorial at Fusilier Bluff. (© Chambers)

Tour 2: Gully Ravine and Beach

This is a short walk that can be accomplished in less than an hour. Its purpose is to give you a feel of Gully Ravine and the hive of activity that would have surrounded the beach area during the campaign.

To find you way to Gully Ravine, leave Seddülbahir village, pass the Helles memorial and Lanchashire Landing Cemetery. Continue on the road past the old post-war Turkish Army camp, Bakery and X Beaches. When the road takes a sudden curve to the right, moving away from the sea, you have arrived. On this corner, if you look towards the sea, you will see a small piece of farmland

HQ of 29th Division on Gully Beach.

'RE 135 COMPANY' clearly marked on the well-head. (© Chambers)

It was so dry that we had to walk over a mile to obtain sufficient water to enable us to drill the holes in readiness for blasting. Day after day we blasted in more ways than one but, having reached a depth of thirty-four feet without even a slightest trace of dampness, we gave it up as hopeless. Imagine our surprise when the engineer-in-charge marked out a spot for another well only a few feet from the white elephant. He said we should have struck water thereabouts and was certain we should be successful with this new well. Strange to say we found traces of dampness almost at once and at four feet had to bale water all the time to get on with the sinking. At six feet the inrush was so hampering our digging that we decided to cut a trench between the two wells so that the water could run into the first one close by. At ten feet we had to abandon all further sinking as we had a supply well and a thirty-four feet container. Our only regret was that it was some distance from the line. We sank several more wells but never quite so successful with this one in the gully...

When you turn your back to the sea, and look at the scrubby bushes above the plateau, there are still various signs of where the troops used to live, gently scarring the ridges. Everywhere on the Peninsula you will find fragments of earthenware rum jars, which make a useful path for following the British in battle, here at Gallipoli and also the Western Front. Some still bear the initials 'S.R.D', officially Supply Reserve Depot, although the troops referred to it as 'Seldom Reaches Destination', amongst many other names. Another legacy of war are the many bullets and bones that are found lying on the surface of the fields or in the nooks and crannies of the ravine, clear evidence of the once heavy fighting in this area.

Although quite stony, the area around the old pier and wrecked lighter is a good place to paddle, when not too rough to swim. Remember how remote this area is and never venture out of your depth. The currents all around the Peninsula can be very dangerous. During the war there were accounts of sharks being spotted, drawn in by the scent of the blood of dead animal carcasses floating in the sea. Today, however, I think you would be lucky to see one. After a long walk the prospect of a cool dip in the Aegean is a welcome treat.

Sketch of Gully Ridge by Captain Guy Nightingale, 1/Royal Munster Fusiliers.

The Ravine

Gully Spur and Gully Ravine are the only areas in the Helles region that resemble the landscape at Anzac. Entering the ravine at Gully Beach, it is approximately a two-mile walk up to the area of the old front line. This is the very same route the troops would have taken during 1915. The mouth of the ravine was a hive of activity during the war, the main communication link for the front line on western part of Helles. Please note tha the pillbox in the gully here, and the ones hidden nearer the beach, are post 1914-1918 war.

An optional twenty minute tour from here is to climb up onto Gully Ridge which gives excellent views across the Helles front and over to the island of Imbros (Sir Ian Hamilton's GHQ) and Samothrace. The ridge was a warren for the troops that lived, slept and died through those now distant months of 1915. In the surrounding scrub there are many remnants of the previous occupation, from broken rum jars, glass bottles and jam tins to the odd bullet and piece of shrapnel. Return carefully back into the gully and proceed back to your vehicle.

But here I dream it no disgrace,
When Sol sits down in Samothrace,
And Father Achi hides his face,
To fill my flask with rum.
Sub-Lieutenant Aubrey P Herbert (Hawke Bn., RND)

Gully Ridge today. (© Chambers)

Tour 3: Gully Ravine and Pink Farm (South)

This is a walk that begins at Pink Farm Cemetery, and takes approximately an hour to complete, taking you over the British reserve area.

Leaving your car at Pink Farm, walk along the road towards Alcitepe (Krithia) for about 400 metres where on the left hand side of the road you will find a rough track leading through the fields towards Gully Ravine. Take this track (made by the British troops and called Artillery Road) and follow the path

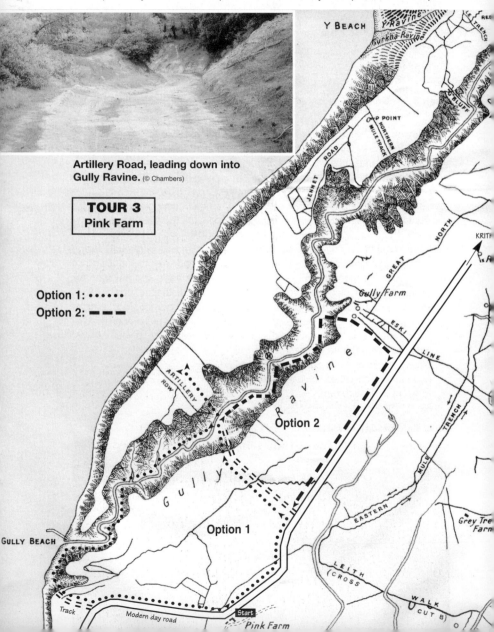

Artillery Road, leading down into Gully Ravine. (© Chambers)

TOUR 3
Pink Farm

Option 1: ••••••
Option 2: ▬ ▬ ▬

Artillery Row, leading up onto Gully Spur. (© Chambers)

down into Gully Ravine. It will take about 10 minutes in total from Cemetery to reach the ravine. As Reverend Oswin Creighton describes:

> I went along the West Krithia road, past the Pink Farm, and then into a deep gully leading towards the firing line. When I had got the horses down into it, I left them with the groom and started to walk up the gully.

We follow the same route today.

A few metres away on the seaward bank of the ravine, almost opposite, is another path that leads up onto Gully Spur. This path was called Artillery Row during the war, and allowed artillery pieces to be positioned on the ridge. It will take approximately eight minutes to reach the top; although a little steep, you will be rewarded with good views along the top of Gully Spur and the sea. The remains of trenches, shell holes and the gun pits can still be traced on this ridge, although they are now heavily overgrown by dense scrub. Beware as the scrub disguises many small holes and rocks that can easily send one falling. A sprained ankle is the last thing you want in this remote region. You have two options when you return to the gully.

Option 1: Head south towards the beach, about 500 metres away and then follow *Tour 2: Gully Ravine and Beach* for the rest of the walk, returning to Pink Farm via the modern road.

Option 2: Head north along the ravine towards the Eski lines passing the sites of the Aberdeen Gully dressing station and Gully Farm. The New Zealanders had a dressing station at the farm during May, and later this became the base of the 1/Field Company, RE. The New Zealanders:

> eventually arrived near a small stone farmhouse on the right hand side

The slope from Gully Ravine up to the Eski Lines, September 1915.

Remains of the Eski trenches today. (© Chambers)

of the gully. On both sides of the road were some old Turkish trenches, in a filthy condition. Sticking up in the parapet was a dead man's hand, like a stop sign, seeming to indicate 'this far and no farther' [4].

Nothing today appears to remain of this farm. Head back to the main road via the site of the Eski lines. This was the major communication trench that connected Gully Ravine over to the eastern side of the Helles battlefield. During 1915 a rumour was started by one of the men that Eski was the pet name of the wife of one of the Staff Officers, to everyone's amusement. Most other trench names were self-explanatory, but Eski was so different nobody really knew what it meant. However the word *eski* is Turkish for old, so 'Old Line' is more likely the realistic origins of the name (approximate front line before the Second Battle of Krithia), some of which are still possible to find today on the eastern side of the modern day road. The headquarters of 88 and 156 Brigade, for the 28 June attacks, were side by side in these lines.

After you have exited the ravine at Gully Farm/Eski line, the slope takes you onto a rough track from where you can then walk back to the main road and Pink Farm.

A concrete well head near the Eski lines. (© Chambers)

Tour 4: Gully Ravine and Twelve Tree Copse (Centre)

This walk takes about two hours, starting at Twelve Tree Copse Cemetery, covering the Fir Tree Spur area, where 156 Brigade attacked on 28 June.

Leaving Twelve Tree Copse Cemetery, head in a southwesterly direction along the road, for about 100 metres, towards Fir Tree Wood. Take the track that heads in a northwesterly direction towards Gully Ravine and the sea. You will cross Engineer Gully, and the sites of the RND Engineer Bivouac Dump, Holborn Circus and Church Farm. When the track runs out, carefully skirt the outer edge of the field, avoiding any crops, and head towards Gully Ravine. It will take approximately five to ten minutes to reach the crest of the ravine.

Walking along the field/tree line of the gully towards it in a northeasterly direction along the ravine top. You will pass above the Zig-Zag and over the sites of the British trench lines of Lancashire Street, Fusilier Street and Frith Walk trenches. The jumping off points for 156 Brigade attack on 28 June were forward of these positions. There are still some well preserved trenches in the

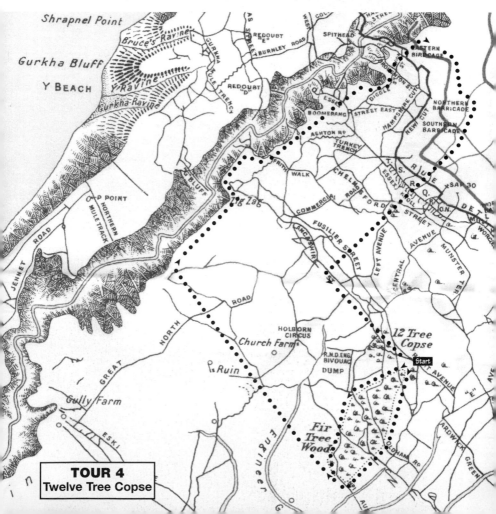

A deep Turkish trench and bombing sap at the site of the Birdcage. (© Chambers)

Part of Frith Walk trench today. (© Chambers)

The Zig-Zag, photographed from the trenches that remain near its crest. (© Chambers)

FUSILIER STREET   ACHI BABA   LANCASHIRE STREET

The Boomerang today. (© Chambers)

woods here, that are in the area of the Zig-Zag. Be careful when following these trench lines, as it is an eighty-foot drop to the bottom of the gully. Return to the edge of the gully/fields and continue to follow the gully line. Little remains today of the old 28 June frontline, now mostly just cultivated fields.

Continuing along the ravine, very soon you will see a patch of rough, uneven ground, covered in thick scrub, between the ravine and fields. This is the site of the infamous Boomerang, captured by the Border Regiment on 28 June. Continue over the sites of Essex, Union and Broughton Street trenches and then onto the Eastern Birdcage, the Gridiron and Border Barricade. This area witnessed heavy trench fighting, mainly by bomb and mine, where you can find good remains of Turkish trenches, preserved in the area of the Birdcage. There are also remains of mine craters, one most probably being Cawley's Crater, still visible, but now covered in thick scrub. Notice what could be a bombing sap in the Turkish trench. Both Turkish and British trenches here were originally covered overhead with chicken wire to stop the bombs raining down within:

> Over the top of the trench we had wire netting, not to keep out the Turk but only his bombs. The trenches were very close at this point. Most of the bombs bounced off the netting but some got spiteful and came right through it. What a scramble when they did![5]

Following the field border, walk in an easterly direction onto Fir Tree Spur ridge,

Panoramic view from Gully Ravine over to Fir Tree Wood. (© Chambers)

GULLY RAVINE   FUSILIER BLUFF   NULLAH
(NURI YAMUT)

The extreme right of the Royal Scots advance on 28 June 1915. This is the approximate position reached by CSM Lowe. (© Chambers)

until you reach a track. Bear to the left and continue along the track until you reach a junction with another track heading in a southerly direction. If you carry on the original path you will come out at Alçitepe, so follow the southerly track back towards Twelve Tree Copse Cemetery. This path takes you over the site of the Turkish 'H' trenches. As you continue you will notice that you are going down a slight gradient, the area where the Cameronians made their fatal attack. In the surrounding fields were the sites of Sap 29 and 30, where Brigadier-General Scott-Moncrieff was killed, and his 156 Brigade decimated. When you are far enough along the track you will see the familiar sight of the distinctive 'Twelve Trees' in the cemetery, which will guide you back safely to your start point.

Tour 5: Fusilier Bluff to Y Beach (North)

The walk will take approximately three hours to complete, beginning at the Turkish Nuri Yamut Memorial at Fusilier Bluff, and taking you over the British and Turkish lines on Gully Spur.

When the crops have been harvested around the Nuri Yamut memorial you can look in the southerly direction and still see the slight rises of what would have been the Turkish and British frontlines. Note a large hole in the field that is positioned over the old British frontline trench; maybe a mine crater or a collapsed dugout or trench? Take the field track that runs from the memorial towards the Nullah. this track roughly runs along the top of the Turkish frontline trench (J.13), before skirting the top end of Gully Ravine.

Continue along the top of the gully into the British lines until you get to the distinctive area of the Zig-Zag and the flat area known as Geoghegan's Bluff or 'G' Bluff, the site of the main cemetery during the war. Leave the crest of the ravine and by carefully skirting the cultivated fields, walk over to Gurkha Bluff on the coast. Down below is Y Beach, also known as Gurkha Beach, locally named Pinarcik Koyu (Little Fountain Cove).

Y Ravine is now completely overgrown, containing a lot of thick prickly scrub over broken ground. The steep descent down to the beach is potentially

170

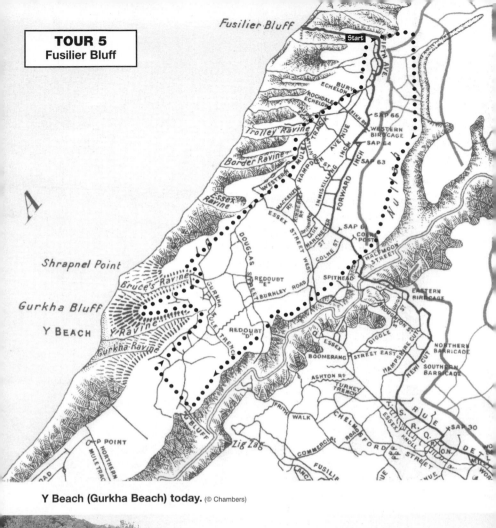

TOUR 5
Fusilier Bluff

Fusilier Bluff

Start

Fifty Ave

BURY ECHELON

ROCHDALE ECHELON

Trolley Ravine

Border Ravine

Essex Ravine

SAP 66

WESTERN BIRDCAGE

SAP 64

SAP 63

BIRN ST

INNISKILLING INCH

HAMPDEN AVENUE

FORWARD INCH

NULLAH

WESTERN MULE TRACK

MACKENZIE ST

GREEN ST

MANCHESTER ST

CATHEDRAL

INNISKILLING ST

COLNE ST

SAP 61

COFFEE POST

Shrapnel Point

Bruce's Ravine

Gurkha Bluff

Y BEACH

Y Ravine

Gurkha Ravine

DOUGLAS STREET WEST

ESSEX STREET WEST

REDOUBT "E"

BURNLEY ROAD

GURKHA MULE TRENCH

REDOUBT

HALFMOON STREET

SPITHEAD

EASTERN BIRDCAGE

BOOMERANG

ESSEX STREET EAST

DIGGLE

HAMPSHIRE CUT

NEW CUT

NORTHERN BARRICADE

SOUTHERN BARRICADE

ASHTON RD

TURKEY TRENCH

SURVEYOR'S CUT

O.P. POINT

NORTHERN MULE TRACK

JC BLUFF

Zig Zag

FRITH WALK

CHELMSFORD ROAD

COMMERCIAL ROAD

LANC

FUSILI

T.C.S. R.Q.

DET

ESSEX KNOLL STREET

R.Q.

SAP 30

ION

WILL

WOR

Y Beach (Gurkha Beach) today. (© Chambers)

Map 23. Turkish trench map of the area between Geoghigans and Fusilier Bluff, December 1915. (Royal Engineers Museum)

Deep remains of British trenches near Gurkha Bluff. (© Chambers)

The deep remains of Gurkha Mule Trench, near Gurkha Bluff. (© Chambers)

hazardous so is not recommended. If you did want to go fighting your way down through the scrub, much of which is fairly impenetrable, this would take you around twenty minutes before reaching the beach. If you decide to take this route follow the dried watercourse that runs down the middle of the ravine, once a communication track linking the beach to the trenches. At the head of Y Ravine was the site of a British Advanced Dressing Station and small cemetery, were a path was used to evacuate the wounded down to the safety of the beach. Another, and equally difficult way is to walk to the seaward tip of Gurkha Bluff and descend down to the beach from there. Not for the faint hearted and extremely hazardous, so think twice. You may find the descent, although extremely steep with many loose rocks and earth, the better way down taking about fifteen minutes, but when you reach the bottom the ascent is a lot tougher. The other gullies in the area are no easier. In the War Diary for the 5/Wiltshire Regiment it is recorded that during the night of the 18/19 July two men[6] were killed by falling rocks near this area. No more casualties are needed!

Please also note that the area is uninhabited, so Do Not do this walk alone.

Rations being taken up Y Ravine, November 1915.

Another possible way to Y Beach is to walk along the coastline, beneath the cliffs from Gully Beach. Again, this is not recommended, as you will have a 2.5 km struggle over fallen rocks, many boulder sized, forcing you to hop from one to another. Y Ravine is recognisable when you get there, as it is the first substantial gully in the cliffs; lying before it is the beach, which is roughly a narrow hundred-metre strip of sand.

Trolley Ravine today. (© Chambers)

Those sensible ones who do not want to make the descent, and wise they are, can get a good view from Gurkha Bluff to the beach below. Gurkha Bluff, heroically captured by 6/Gurkhas in May 1915, later served as the headquarters for 126 Brigade (42nd Division) and the attached South Eastern Mounted Brigade.

A drawing of a post in Trolley Ravine

Water supply at Bruce's Ravine, October 1915. (WSRC RSR PH 7/11)

During the Gully Ravine fighting in June, 108 and 87/Field Ambulances (29th Division) had their dressing stations based here. Wounded were evacuated down onto the beach, and along the seashore road for embarkation at Gully Beach. Walk along the cliff top, skirting the crops and be careful along the edge, as this can be quite dangerous and crumbly in places. From Gurkha Bluff you will pass Bruce's Ravine, named after Colonel Bruce, 6/Gurkhas, and the area where the Royal Munster Fusiliers assembled for the 28 June attack. In the area of Shrapnel Point there is some woodland that contains deep remains of Gurkha Mule Trench. Even though there are cultivated fields between here and the gully, the exit of this trench is still traceable as it descends into the ravine. Continue along the cliff to Essex Ravine, where the Mushroom Redoubt was positioned, Border Ravine and Trolley Ravine. To the right of Trolley Ravine, would have been trench J.12 and the position known as Inniskilling Inch, where the two Irish VCs were won. Continue past the Echelons (Salford, Rochdale and Bury), and return to Fusilier Bluff. A battlefield visitor in the 1930s recalled:

> I came to Salford, Rochdale, and Bury Echelons, disturbing a snake on my way. Behind the echelons, Sikh Road led to the Western Bridcage and various saps. Litter was thick round the Echelons. There were bombs, periscopes, tin linings of S.A.A. boxes, mess-tins, Maconochie tins, other tins, rum-jars – broken or whole, but empty – curls of barbed wire, a sniper's shield, pick heads, shovels, a long, thin bayonet bent and twisted, rotten leather pouches and scabbards, shell cases, bullets, shrapnel balls, iron splinters, rifle-barrels, and some water-bottle corks whose deficiency-returns used to be demanded by unimaginative Staff-Captains at inconvenient times.[7]

Tour 6: Gully Ravine – the Big Walk

The big walk will take the whole day, about seven hours, there and back. This is based on walking at a leisurely pace, with a few short stops for a rest, a drink of water and scurry into the odd side gully. Although the path you follow is not always very wide, and here and there almost non-existent, the going is never very tough. It is advisable to take plenty of water with you during the summer months, and some food. There is no civilisation at all in this area.

Border Barricade, the old gully frontline, is the goal, taking you a leisurely two and a half hours. If you want to investigate the many little side gullies and ravines running off from both sides, and generally wander around, allow more time. Along the route you can still come across numerous signs of trench warfare, from broken rum jars, mess tins, rusting bully beef tins, the odd button or bullet, numerous pieces of shrapnel and sometimes bones. The walls of the ravine still show remains that would have once been dugouts and

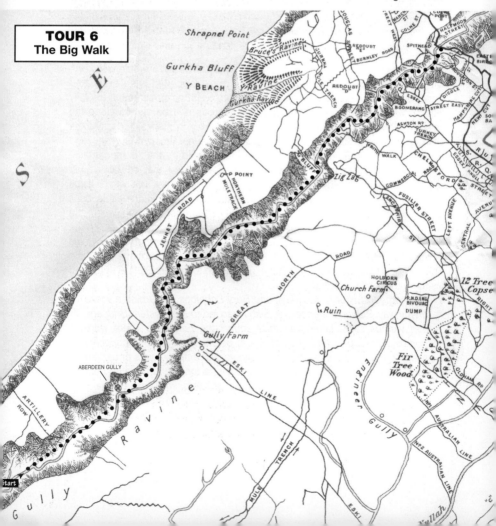

trenches, although many of these have long since been washed away. Surprisingly though, there is still a lot to see in Gully Ravine from the 1915 period, preserved to a degree by the remoteness of this region.

Tip: If you only want to walk the one way, taking under three hours, it is possible to arrange for a taxi to wait for you either at the Nuri Yamut Turkish memorial at Fusilier Bluff, or alternatively at Gully Beach. If you can manage to walk both ways, this adds greatly to the Gully Ravine experience and overall ambience of what must be one of the most beautiful parts of the battlefield.

Entering Gully Ravine from the beach you will soon notice, once inside the mouth, that the sea breeze suddenly stops, and the heat and silence of the enclosed gully then hits you:

> The Gully is a strange and disturbing place, if ghosts walk anywhere
> they walk in Gully Ravine.[8]

This part of the ravine is fairly wide, but soon the walls close in on you, tall and steep. See *Tour 2: Gully Ravine and Beach* for details of this area.

Approximately one kilometre (twenty minutes) inland, you come to an open space of about 3000 square meters. Towards the end of this open space, at the right hand eastern, side, there is a dirt track going up to Fir Tree Spur. This is Artillery Road, built by the British in 1915, leading to Pink Farm, which will take you back to the modern road that you originally left when entering Gully Beach. Almost opposite the track on the western side of the Ravine another old track leads up onto Gully Spur, this was called Artillery Row. At the top of this track the British located some of their gun batteries. It is still impossible to walk up this path, although a little steep, which rewards you with good views along the top of Gully Spur. The remains of trenches and the gun positions can still be traced, although overgrown by dense scrub. See *Tour 3: Gully Ravine and Pink Farm* for further details of this area.

Return to the Ravine by the same track and continue along the streambed. Walk for another 300 metres (six minutes) where you will find two fairly large offspring ravines on the left-hand side of the gully. These are the sites of the former British dressing stations of 88 and 89/Field Ambulances (29th Division), established within these gullies in June 1915. The first one was called Aberdeen Gully after the hometown of the 89/Field Ambulance. In Creighton's diary entry for 14 June, he remarks:

> ...about 500 yards from the firing line in a little gully called Aberdeen
> Gully (as the 89th come from there), which runs off the big gully. A
> narrow path about fifty yards long had been cut out of the bed formed
> by a stream, now dry. The path runs up into a little natural amphitheatre
> in the cliff, about fifteen yards in diameter. The sides of the gully are
> almost precipitous, but it had been widened enough at places to make a
> dressing-station, cookhouse, and officers' mess, and the amphitheatre is
> also used as a dressing station if necessary...At the 89th we succeeded
> in making a very snug dressing-station in Aberdeen Gully, where the
> patients might be secure and undisturbed while shells burst overhead.

The 88/Field Ambulance used the gully next door, where Creighton goes on to recall his experience during the Turkish counterattack on 5 July:

Aberdeen Gully. (© Chambers)

> ...about 3.45 we were awakened by a most terrific bombardment, which did not really stop till 10.30. In this little gully it is impossible to know what is happening. It seemed as though we were sending the most shells over at first. And then the Turks sent more and more. They simply flew over in hundreds. I think we are almost absolutely secure in here. But shells came as close as possible. Two Jack Johnsons fell in the 88th gully next door, and one blew their kitchen to pieces. But they could not get us.

Approximately 300 metres (six minutes) further along, on the right, you pass a wooded, wide open, slope that takes you into what used to be the Eski Lines, and the site of Gully Farm, up on Fir Tree Spur. There used to be a supply dump here, used by the Royal Engineers and the Sussex Yeomanry later on in the campaign. The Eski lines served as major lines of communication over to the eastern side of the battlefield.

Many of the other small offshoot gullies sheltered everything from Indian and Zion Mule Corps mules to cookhouses, stores, ammunition dumps and field dressing posts. There even sprang up a small Divisional School where they constructed a thirty-yard rifle range and held bombing classes, both giving useful experience to newly arrived reinforcements. Continuing up the ravine, on the left hand side would have been communication trenches leading up onto Gully Spur. Northern Mule Track joined up with Western Mule Trench, which was dug wide enough for mules to taken provisions to the Y Beach area.

If you continue for almost a kilometre (twenty minutes) you arrive at the area immediately behind the front line of 28 June 1915. On the left there is a flat piece of ground, easy to miss, about eight metres from the bottom of the ravine. Ascending onto this terrace will bring you onto the area known as Geoghegan's Bluff or 'G' Bluff. The high ravine wall opposite is the Zig-Zag. During the war it had an old goat track, which zigged and zagged down its

Relic of war – a British blue enamelled water bottle, found in Gully Ravine. (© Chambers)

Relic of war – the top of a water tin dated 1915. (© Chambers)

Geoghegan's Bluff and cemetery in October 1915. (WSRC RSR PH 7/11)

face, a route that took the troops to and from the trenches. The headquarters of 125 and 127 Brigades (42nd Division) were based here, as well as the forward base for VIII Corps mining companies:

> Those who lived on the Gully sides in 1915 would hardly know their old homes now, for only slight traces of dug-outs and shelters can be seen; but there are other signs of occupation, and, on a slope near the Zig-Zag, I found buttons from British tunics, webbing, broken rum-jars, and shrapnel and bullets from both sides. In the Turkish gullylines, between Krithia and Fusilier Bluff, two large and live shells lay by the side of the stream; and close by I came to a clean trench, 10 feet deep and crossable only where the sides had given way...Today, Geoghegan's Bluff and the Boomerang are deserted; and are places without meaning to the few local people who pass them.[9]

From here you have two options, either exit at Geoghegan's Bluff (Option 1), or continue on to Border Barricade and the Nullah (Option 2) through the ravine.

Option 1: Crossing the fields from Geoghegan's Bluff will take you over to Y Ravine, taking approximately another fifteen minutes. See *Tour 5: Fusilier Bluff to Y Beach*, for further details. When you reach Fusilier Bluff either retrace your path and return to Gully Beach, or re-enter Gully Ravine, and walk back

Geoghegan's Bluff today. (© Ohambaro)

Geoghegan's Bluff Plot. (© Chambers)

Geoghegan's Bluff look over to the Zig-Zag. (© Chambers)

from the direction of the Turkish lines, down pass Border Barricade, and then Gully Beach.

Option 2: Continue on from Geoghegan's Bluff through the ravine. Passing the Zig-Zag, on the left-hand bank, you will notice the remains of Gurkha Mule Trench that leads up onto Gully Spur. This trench is still fairly accessible, and well worth making a short detour along. Further along you will soon come to some stone and earthwork remains in the area of Redoubt 'C', that leads up into Frith Walk, the frontline for 28 June. Continuing along, up on the right hand side are the sites of the Boomerang and Turkey Trenches. The trench lines of Essex Street West and Essex Street East are also fairly easily located, and still accessible from the ravine. Continue on to Border Barricade. If you reach an open flattish area you have gone too far. The remains of Border Barricade comprises of

The exit from the ravine onto Geoghegan's Bluff. (© Chambers)

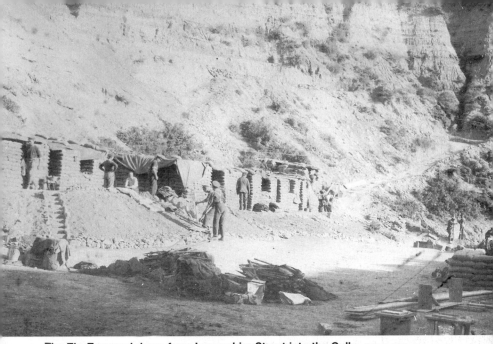

The Zig-Zag road down from Lancashire Street into the Gully. (IWM Q14849)

rough dry-stone reinforcements to the earth banks and some scrub covered trenches. This was the British front line after 28 June, through to the evacuation. When you pass this area, you will realise that the cliffs on the left start getting a lot shallower, and from the open area it is best to exit the ravine and head along the top of the western bank to Fusilier Bluff and the Turkish Nuri Yamut Memorial.

At this point you have several options for your return, assuming that you have not arranged for a taxi to pick you up. To extend your walk you can either

The Zig-Zag today. (Chambers)

Gurkha Mule Trench leading up from Gully Ravine. (© Chambers)

Remains of Redoubt 'C', looking north, Frith Walk to the right. This was the old British front line on the morning of 28 June. (© Chambers)

Turkish photo of Border Barricade after the evacuation.

The same view today. (Chambers)

Another Turkish photo of the barricaded ravine from a different angle.

Returning from the lines, down the Zig-Zag. (IWM Q61085)

return to Gully Beach the way you came, or follow *Tour 4: Gully Ravine and Twelve Tree Copse,* returning to your vehicle via Pink Farm and the main road.

If I should die, think only this of me:
That there's some corner of a foreign field
That is forever England. There shall be
In that rich earth a richer dust concealed;
A dust whom England bore, shaped, made aware,
A body of England's breathing English air,
Washed by the rivers, blest by suns of home.

And think, this heart, all evil shed away,
A pulse in the eternal mind, no less
Give somewhere back the thoughts by England given;
Her sights and sounds; dreams happy as her day;
And laughter, learnt of friends; and gentleness,
In hearts at peace, under an English heaven.

'The Soldier' by Sub-Lieutenant Rupert Brook, Hood Btn., RND (1887-1915)

1. Pemberton, T. J. *Gallipoli To-Day,* (1926)
2. Murray, Joseph, *Gallipoli As I Saw It,* (1965), p.162.
3. Sergeant, J. N. B. 'With The French Artillery', *The Gallipolian,* No. 67, Christmas 1991, p.20.
4. Waite, Major Fred, DSO, *The New Zealanders at Gallipoli,* (1921), pp.123-124.
5. Murray, *Op. Cit.,* p.158.
6. Private Frank Baden, 9413 and Private Frank Gough, 9409, both are buried in Pink Farm Cemetery.
7. 'The Silent Nullahs of Gallipoli'. *Twenty Years After, The Battlefields of 1914-1918: Then and Now,* Volume II, p.1226.
8. Sellers, Leonard, 'Incident at Gully Ravine', *RND Magazine,* No.2, September 1997, p.139.
9. 'The Silent Nullahs of Gallipoli', *Op. Cit.,* p. 1224

Appendix I

1. Artillery Bombardment

At 9 A.M. on the 28th instant a heavy artillery bombardment will commence on the Turkish position.

At 10.20 A.M. this will be followed by a bombardment by field artillery with a view to cutting wire entanglements in front of Turkish trenches.

During intervals of artillery bombardment, concentrated enfilade fire from three machine-gun batteries will be directed along J.9, J.10, J.11 and H.11, as well as up the Ravine as far as the junction of the Ravine and Nullah.

At 10.40 A.M. another heavy bombardment will be carried out, and at 11 A.M. ranges will be lengthened and direction altered on to H.14 and J.12.

2. 1st Infantry Assault

At 11 A.M. exactly, all watches having been previously checked under divisional arrangements, the companies detailed for assault will spring forward on the order 'Attack' from company commanders, which will be repeated all along the line by platoon and section commanders.

The 156th Brigade will assault H.12a, H.12, H.11 and the Nullah north-east of H.11 as far as the communicating trench joining H.12 at the bend of the Nullah.

The 87th Brigade will assault J.9, J.10, J.11 and half J.11a; also the Boomerang Trench east of the Ravine and that part of the Ravine held by the enemy as far as J.11.

At the same time the Indian Brigade will advance from its position, west of the left sub-section fire trenches, along the cliffs between the crest and the sea, and will take over from the 87th Brigade and occupy, J.11a, from J.11 to a point about half-way to J.12, establishing itself upon this line to protect the left flank of the skirmishers of the 87th Brigade and the front of J.11 while this is being consolidated. The remainder of the attacking portion of the brigade will be collected below the left flank of this line preparatory for a further advance.

As soon as H.12 and J.11 have been captured, this line will be joined and consolidated with the utmost rapidity.

3. 2nd Infantry Assault

At 11.30 A.M., failing orders to the contrary, the 86th Bde. will advance in echelon from the left against J.11a, J.12, and J.13. This attack across the open under cover of the artillery bombardment of J.12, J.13 and H.14 will be carried out as rapidly as is consistent with maintaining the troops fit to assault. It will also be assisted by the Indian Brigade, who will advance up J.11a, and between that trench and the sea, and will be responsible for the left flank of the 86th Brigade. When the 86th Brigade reaches its objective, the Indian Brigade will hold a line from the N.W. end of J.13 to the sea.

The Indian Brigade will also detail sufficient men to occupy J.11a as a fire trench facing East.
As soon as J.12 and 13 have been captured, these trenches will be placed in a state of defence. The Field Company R.E. attached to the 86th Brigade will assist in joining the Eastern ends of J.13 and J.12, and from there in the direction of the double bend in the Ravine between J.10a and H.12. The Field Company R.E. attached to the 87th Brigade will assist in preparing trenches from this point of the Ravine in a northerly direction to connect with those of the 86th Brigade. This line of trenches will be sited according to the ground so as to meet a counter-attack from the direction of H.14. This line cannot be continuous, but will be dug in lengths of about 100 yards, which will be connected as soon as possible by sapping, and the trenches as soon as ready for occupation will be manned by troops sent up from the 86th and 87th Brigades.

4. Divisional Reserve

When the assault takes place the 88th Brigade will hold our present line, between the 42nd Division on the right and Gully Ravine inclusive on the left. The Indian Brigade reserves will hold from the Gully Ravine exclusive to the sea. The strength of this line will be 1 man to 4 yards.

Eight machine guns from the 86th and 87th Brigades, under Brigade Machine Gun Officers, and six machine guns from the Royal Naval Motor Maxim Squadron, will be established as three batteries in suitable positions to enfilade J.10, J.11, and H.11 prior to the first assault. After the 1st assault Brigade Machine-Gun Batteries will be at the disposal of the 86th and 87th Brigades if required. The remainder of the machine guns will be at the disposal of battalions, under brigade arrangements, to defend trenches gained.

The artillery supporting the attack will always be ready to establish a barrage de feu on the front and flanks of the attacking infantry, especially between H.14 and the Ravine.

5. General Instructions

1. Arrangements will be made by brigades to enable every man to know exactly what he has to do, whether he belongs to the assaulting party, the supporting party, or to the consolidating party.

2. Scaling ladders will be provided, and sally ports and steps on the front side of the present firing trenches will be prepared, so that assaulting columns can emerge from the firing trenches easily and quickly on the command 'Attack'.

3. One Field Company R.E. will be attached to the 156th Brigade, one to the 87th Brigade, and a third to the 86th Brigade. A small party of the R.E.'s must be distributed among the assaulting companies, with special duty, after an enemy's trench has been captured, of searching for and cutting all wires which may be leading to mines, and to destroy any mines which may be found.

4. Columns will be organized into:-
> *Assaulting Parties.*
> *Supports with Bombing Parties on the flanks.*
> *Reserves.*

5. Each Battn. will be provided with two screens, red with a white diagonal on one side and khaki on the other. They will be erected by day in rear of trenches to indicate to artillery that supporting fire is required. By night Battn. Hqrs. will keep six Very Pistols and indicate the same request for support by clusters of six lights fired simultaneously. These demands for fire support must not be made without sufficient cause. The Very Pistols are only intended to supplement telephones if out of order.

6. Each man of assaulting companies will carry on his back an equilateral triangular piece of biscuit tin, 1 foot wide, connected by two loops of string to the shoulders. These triangles to be used under the orders of the Platoon Commanders for marking the extent of the advance, a proportion of them being erected in the back of any trench gained. Packs will not be carried. Assaulting parties will carry entrenching implements, but will not carry entrenching tools. Support and Reserve parties will carry these in the proportion of three shovels to one pick, shovels being tied across the back. All troops will carry two empty sand-bags through the waistbelt, and will carry 200 rounds S.A.A., one day's iron rations, and full water bottles.

7. As each trench is captured it will at once be placed in a state of defence. For this purpose parties will be detailed beforehand.

All communication trenches leading from the enemy towards captured trenches will be occupied and barricaded by parties detailed beforehand, about 50 yards in advance of all captured trenches. These points, together with a few skirmishers pushed forward, will form a covering party under which the work of consolidation will be carried out.

Communication trenches between our present line and captured trenches will be at once prepared or improved by parties detailed beforehand from the Brigades in Divisional Reserve holding our present line.

8. All troops are reminded that the care of wounded falls to the duty of Field Ambulances. No fighting troops are to accompany wounded men to Dressing Stations. Police Posts will be established by the Provost Marshal to see this order is not disobeyed and that no one leaves the front line without orders.

9. Brigades are responsible that in no case are copies of Divisional, Brigade, or Battalion Orders to be in the hands of anyone holding the front-line trenches, as the capture of an officer or man in possession of these orders would render the whole operation abortive.

General Officer Commanding 87th Brigade:
The objectives allotted to the 87th Bde. Are:-

The Boomerang Fort and that portion of the Turkey Trench still in the hands of the enemy.
The Gully Ravine as far as its junction with J.11.
J.9 – J.10 – J.11 and half J.11a.

2. During the bombardment our present firing trenches extending from the Turkey Trench inclusive to the west end of the Indian Brigade line, together with such supporting trenches and nullahs in rear of this frontage as may be required, are allotted to the 87th Brigade. The 87th Brigade will be formed up in these trenches preparatory to delivering the assault. Troops not required for the assault, etc., should be kept in the Gully Ravine in Brigade Reserve.
The various portions of the Brigade will be formed up in their respective positions by 9.0 A.M. No troops will be placed in the firing trench of the Indian Brigade owing to the nearness of their trench to J.9 and the consequent danger of blowbacks from our own artillery.

3. As successive lines emerge from our present firing line, their places will be taken by succeeding lines ready to advance as the situation demands, so as to make room as soon as possible for the 86th Brigade, who will eventually attack beyond J.11 through the 87th Brigade.

4. The consolidation of the J.11 line up to the Gully Ravine inclusive must be executed with the utmost rapidity, as the attack of the 86th Bde. cannot be launched until that line is safe against counter-attack from the east, and the time during which that Brigade can advance under cover of the artillery bombardment is limited to one hour from the time of the launching of the assault of the 87th Brigade. The early intimation of the consolidation of the J.11 line to the G.O.C. 86th Brigade is thus of the utmost importance.

5. 87th Brigade Headquarters will be established at the same place as 86th Brigade Headquarters.

6. Much depends on the success of the 86th Brigade assault and its ability to maintain the positions won. Your Brigade must be prepared to assist as much as possible by seizing and preparing for defence advanced positions between the double bend of the Ravine north of H.11 and J.12.

A few machine guns sent up to tactical points of this line will be of the greatest value.

General Officer Commanding 156th Brigade:

1. The task of capturing H.12 line allotted to the Brigade has on previous occasions proved easy. Failure to retain possession has been due to want of support on the left of that line, which will now be forthcoming. To make it successful on this occasion the task of each company, platoon and section must be worked out in detail beforehand.

2. The Brigade will be formed up in the fire trenches of the·right sub-section and of the centre sub-section to the Turkey Trench exclusive by 8 A.M. Portions of battalions told off to assault will be in front with R.E. parties. Behind these will be supports, digging, and R.E. parties carrying tools as directed. The exact position of each with a view to easy advance will be selected beforehand after careful reconnaissance and compass bearings to the front to be assaulted.

3. The length of the objective H.12a – H12 – H.11 and the Ravine North-east of H.11 as far as the communicating trench joining H.12 at the bend of the Ravine, will be calculated from the diagram, and the strength of the various portions of the attack will be calculated as follows:-

        1 man per yard for assaulting party
        $^1/^2$ man per yard for supporting party (includes diggers)
        $^1/^2$ man per yard for reserve.

4. Particular attention will be paid to the defence of Gully Ravine against a probable counter-attack from the direction of H.14. Machine guns would probably be usefully employed to enfilade the Gully from Left of H.12.

5. As soon as the captured trenches have been consolidated attention will be paid to the improvements of communications.

6. It is anticipated that the artillery bombardment on this occasion, which is more intense than any in Flanders in support of our troops, will render the task of the brigade easy. More-over, the 88th Brigade will be in the main trenches in close support.

7. The greatest difficulty will probably be found in the capture of H.11 and the double bend of the Ravine north of it, and this task should be allotted to a selected battalion.

8. It must be impressed on all ranks that men must not stop to fire, but rush forward using the bayonet.

The G.O.C. feels sure that the 156th Brigade will show the same fighting spirit as the Lowland Battalion which he has the honour to command, and that he will be able to congratulate the 156th Brigade on the capture and retention of the Turkish trenches allotted to it as objective.

Instructions for R.N. Co-operation

1. Time to be used for the operations will be Military Time, which will be communicated by the Staff Officer, Indian Brigade, who will embark on H.M.S. 'Wolverine' with a signal party at 8.0 A.M. at Gully Beach. Throughout these operations H.M.S. 'Wolverine' will be kept in close touch by signal with the foremost troops of the Indian Brigade as well as with Headquarters of the 87th Brigade.

2. The bombardment will commence at 9.0 A.M. from the sea as well as from land.

H.M.S. Wolverine & Scorpion. Until 11 A.M. H.M.S. 'Wolverine' and 'Scorpion' will divide the front along the top of the cliff from J.9 to the letters J.11a, and will bombard the Turkish trenches about 2' below the crest all along this line with 12-pdr., and the 4" guns of both destroyers will be concentrated on the Redoubt at North-West end of J.11.

H.M.S. Talbot. Until 11 A.M. H.M.S. 'Talbot' will bombard the crest from the letters J.11a to J.13, subjecting the trench to heavy fire and enfilading J.12 and J.13. The cliff crest from J.13 to Sari Tepe will also be bombarded with less intensity, and a strict watch kept on Sari Tepe in case gun fire is opened from there on the Indian Brigade.

3. The assault on J.10 – J.11 and the south-western half of J.11a will be delivered at 11. A.M. and the most intense fire will be delivered just before that hour. From that hour onward fire will be directed on trenches J.12 and J.13.

After the capture of J.11 the Indian Brigade will advance along J.11a, and under the crest, on the left of the 86th Brigade, and H.M.S. 'Wolverine' will be informed by helio signal from the Naval Observation Station when to cease fire. The signal, CF repeated many times, will be made when the 86th Brigade crosses J.11 to assault J.12. Fire will then be directed to points more to the north-east and east at any points from which Turkish fire can be expected.

General Officer Commanding 88th Infantry Brigade:
In the attack on 28th instant the 156th Brigade will attack H.12 and H.11.

To enable them to get into position the 156th Brigade will occupy the front line of trenches now held by your Brigade, from the junction of H.12 with our present firing line as far West as the Turkey Trench south-west of H.11.

The troops you withdraw from this line can be accommodated in the Nullahs south of the Mule Track, or other suitable positions, and you must give the 156th Brigade whatever accommodation they require in your support and reserve trenches as well. This relief will be completed by 6.0 P.M. on the 27th. On the 28th, when the 156th Brigade attacks, their places will then be taken by your Brigade, who will then become responsible that the line from the junction with H.12 to the Gully Ravine inclusive is held lightly – one man to four yards. In addition to this permanent garrison you will maintain units in position as close to the firing line as cover permits, to support the 156th brigade if necessary, and even to carry out the task allotted to that brigade should it, or part of it, fail to accomplish its objective. Should part of that brigade be driven back, you will be responsible that the line is at once regained by counterattack, using the reserves of the 156th Brigade if possible, but if they are not prepared to advance again this must be done by your brigade.

26th June 1915

29TH DIVISIONAL ORDER NO. 8
BY MAJOR-GENERAL H. DE B. DE LISLE, C.B., D.S.O.
COMMANDING 29TH DIVISION

GULLY BEACH, 27th June '15.

1. The Division will attack tomorrow, 28th inst., in accordance with the instructions already issued.

2(a) **S.A. Ammunition Supply**. The following quantities of S.A.A. will be maintained under Brigade arrangements at the undermentioned places, by drawing if necessary upon the main S.A.A. dump, which is established at Pink Farm.

(i) 200 Boxes Mark VII to be maintained by 88th Brigade at a place selected by them.
(ii) 200 Boxes Mark VI in support trenches of right subsection to be maintained by the 156th Brigade.
(iii) 100 Boxes Mark VII in Gully Ravine, near 87th Brigade Headquarters, to be maintained by the 87th Brigade.
(iv) 200 Boxes Mark VII in Gully Ravine, near Geogheghan's Bluff, to be maintained by the Indian Infantry Brigade.

(b) **Very Pistols**. The 87th and 156th Brigades will send down to the dump at Geogheghan's Bluff at daybreak to-morrow, 28th inst., the Very Pistols and ammunition for them, which they have taken over today as trench stores. These will be handed over to the Army Ordnance Corps representative there and will be redistributed under Divisional arrangements.

3. **Medical Arrangements**. The following are the arrangements for the evacuation of wounded during the operations:-

(a) Casualties in the 88th and 156th Brigades and in the right sub-section will be evacuated by the Eastern Mule Track to the Dressing Station to be established by the 88th Field Ambulance about 200 yards north of Pink Farm and about 50 yards west of the West Krithia Road, whence they will be sent direct to Lancashire Landing for embarkation.
(b) Casualties in the 86th and 87th Brigades and in the centre sub-section will be evacuated to the Dressing Station established by the 88th and 89th Field Ambulances in the Gully Ravine, near the Indian Brigade Mule Track, whence they will be sent to Gully Beach for embarkation.
(c) Casualties in the Indian Brigade and among the British on the extreme left will be evacuated to the Dressing Station established by the 108th and 87th Field Ambulances respectively, whence they will be sent along the sea-shore to Gully Beach for embarkation.

4. **Police Arrangements**. Police posts, consisting of three men each, will be established for the operations as follows:-

(a) A post at the junction of the Eski Line and Eastern Mule Track.
(b) A post at the White House on the Eski Line overlooking Gully Ravine.
(c) A post at the junction of the Indian Brigade Mule Track and Gully Ravine.
(d) A post on the beach half-way between Gurkha Bluff and Gully Ravine.

The Police have received strict instructions to turn back all stragglers, and to report their names to the Brigade Headquarters.

Arrangements have been made to supply brigades with camel tanks or water tins, for sending up water to the front, and it will not be necessary to send men to the rear with water bottles to have them filled.

5. **Prisoners of War.** The following are the arrangements for the disposal of prisoners of war, captured during the operation.

(a) Prisoners captured by the 88th and 156th Brigades will be sent under escort to the junction of the Eastern Mule Track and Eski Line, where they will be handed over to a guard of 1 officer and 20 men furnished from the Divisional Cyclist Coy.

(b) Prisoners captured by the 86th, 87th and Indian Brigades will be send under escort to the junction of the Indian Brigade Mule Track and Gully Ravine, where they will be handed over to a guard of 1 officer and 30 men furnished from the Divisional Cyclist Coy.

The prisoners will be marched in batches by the cyclist guards to Lancashire Landing, where they will be handed over to the Commandant, Lancashire Landing.

The guards provided by the Divisional Cyclist Coy. will be in position by 10.30 A.M. on the 28th inst.

6. **Reports.** Brigade Commanders will at once report any events of importance to Divl. Hqrs., and will forward progress reports at every clock hour.

7. **Divisional Headquarters.** Divisional Headquarters will be at Gully Beach up to 9 A.M. and after that hour at the Observation Post east of Gully Ravine.

Issued at 5.0 P.M.   C. J. PERCEVAL, Lieut.-Colonel G.S., 29th Division.

Appendix II

Order of Battle for Gully Ravine, 28 June 1915
Commander-in-Chief: General Sir Ian Hamilton GCB
CGS: Major-General W. P. Braithwaite CB
VIII Corps: Major-General A. G. Hunter-Weston CB

29th Division GOC: Major-General Beauvoir de Lisle

86 Brigade
2/Royal Fusiliers
1/Lancashire Fusiliers
1/Royal Munster Fusiliers
1/Royal Dublin Fusiliers

88 Brigade (Lieutenant-Colonel Cayley)
4/Worcestershire Regiment
2/Hampshire Regiment
1/Essex Regiment
5/Royal Scots (Queen's Edinburgh Rifles) (TF)

156 Brigade (Brigadier-General W. Scott-Moncrieff)
4/Royal Scots (Queen's Edinburgh Rifles)
7/Royal Scots (Leith Rifles) *
7/Cameronians (Scottish Rifles)
8/Cameronians (Scottish Rifles)
* One Company from the 8/Highland Light Infantry attached due to Gretna losses.

87 Brigade (Brigadier-General William Marshall)
2/South Wales Borderers
1/King's Own Scottish Borderers
1/Royal Inniskilling Fusiliers
1/Border Regiment

29 Indian Brigade (Major-General H. V. Cox)
6/Gurkha Rifles
14/Sikhs (King George's Own Ferozepore)
5/Gurkhas Rifles
10/Gurkhas Rifles

Artillery (Brigadier-General Sir Hugh Simpson Baikie)
15 Brigade RHA (B, L, Y Batteries)
17 Brigade RFA (13, 26, 92 Batteries)
147 Brigade RFA (10, 97 and 368 Batteries)

1 (N.S.W) Australian FA Brigade (1, 2, 3 Batteries)
Composite Artillery Brigade consisting of: 6 (Victoria) Australian, 3 New Zealand FA and 6 (East Lancs) Batteries
4 (Highland) Mountain Battery RGA (TF)
14 (Siege) Battery RGA
90 (Heavy) Battery RGA
460 (Howitzer) Battery RFA
4 City of Glasgow (Howitzer) Battery
5 (East Lancs) Battery RFA
and nine French Howitzers and supporting Naval 12 pdrs

Field Ambulance
86/Field Ambulance
87/Field Ambulance
88/Field Ambulance
89/Field Ambulance
108/Indian Field Ambulance

Engineers
2/London Company RE (TF)
2/Lowland Company RE (TF)
1/West Riding Field Company RE (TF)

Divisional Troops
29th Divisional Cyclist Company
RNAS (Motor Maxim Squadrons)

Appendix III

Turkish units in action at Gully Ravine

I Army Corps
Officer Commanding: Mehmed Ali Pasha

3rd Division
Officer Commanding: Halid Bey
31/Infantry Regiment
32/Infantry Regiment
39/Infantry Regiment

II Army Corps
Officer Commanding: Faik Pasha

4th Division
Officer Commanding: Jelal Bey
10/Infantry Regiment
11/Infantry Regiment
12/Infantry Regiment
4/Field Artillery Regiment (7 batteries)
4/Pontoon Section

5th Division
Officer Commanding: Fuad Zia Bey
13/Infantry Regiment
14/Infantry Regiment
15/Infantry Regiment
5/Field Artillery Regiment (6 batteries)
5/Pontoon Section

6th Division
Officer Commanding: Suleiman Shakir Bey
16/Infantry Regiment
17/Infantry Regiment
18/Infantry Regiment
6/Field Artillery Regiment (6 batteries)
6/Pontoon Section

III Army Corps
Officer Commanding: Essad Pasha

9th Division
Officer Commanding: Khalil Sami Bey
25/Infantry Regiment
26/Infantry Regiment
27/Infantry Regiment
9/Field Artillery Regiment (6 batteries)
9/Pontoon Section

IV Army Corps
Officer Commanding: Pertev Pasha

11th Division
Officer Commanding: Rifaat Bey
33/Infantry Regiment
126/Infantry Regiment
127/Infantry Regiment
11/Field Artillery Regiment (6 batteries)
11/Pontoon Section

12th Division
Officer Commanding: Salaheddin Bey
34/Infantry Regiment
35/Infantry Regiment
36/Infantry Regiment
12/Field Artillery Regiment (4 batteries)

189

Bibliography and Recommended Further Reading

Bartlett, E. Ashmead, *Despatches from the Dardanelles*, (London: George Newnes Ltd, 1915).

Behrend, Arthur, *Make Me A Soldier: A Platoon Commander in Gallipoli*, (London: Eyre & Spottiswoode, 1961).

Creighton, Revd O., CF, *With the Twenty Ninth Division: A Chaplain's Experiences*, (London: Longmans, Green & Co., 1916).

Edwards, Lieutenant-Colonel H. I. Powell-, *The Sussex Yeomanry and 16th Battalion Royal Sussex Regiment 1914-1919*, (London: Andrew Melrose, 1921).

Ewing, Major John, *The Royal Scots 1914-1918*, (London: Oliver & Boyd, 1925).

Gibbon, Frederick P. *The 42nd (East Lancashire) Division, 1914-1918*, (London: 1920).

Gillam, Major John Graham, *Gallipoli Diary*, (London: 1918).

Hamilton, General Sir Ian, *Gallipoli Diary*, (London: Edward Arnold, 1920).

Holts, Tonie and Valmai, *Major & Mrs Holt's Battlefield Guide: Gallipoli*, (Barnsley: Leo Cooper, 2000).

James, Robert Rhodes, *Gallipoli*, (London: Pan Books Ltd, 1984).

Mackenzie, Compton, *Gallipoli Memories*, (London: Cassell and Company Ltd, 1929).

Murray, Joseph, *Gallipoli As I Saw It*, (London: William Kimber, 1965).

North, John, *Gallipoli: The Fading Vision*, (London: 1936).

Oglander, Brigadier-General C. F. Aspinall-, *History of the Great War: Military Operations: Gallipoli*, 2 volumes, (London: William Heinemann Ltd, 1929-32).

Patterson, Lieutenant-Colonel J. D., *With the Zionists in Gallipoli*, (New York: 1916).

Pemberton, T. J, *Gallipoli To-Day*, (London: 1926).

Ryan, Major D. G. J, *Historical Record of the 6th Gurkha Rifles, Vol. I 1817-1919*, (1925).

Snelling, Stephen, *VCs of the First World War: Gallipoli*, (Stroud: Alan Sutton, 1995).

Steel, Nigel and Peter Hart, *Defeat at Gallipoli*, (London: Macmillan, 1994).

Steel, Nigel, *Battleground Europe: Gallipoli*, (Barnsley: Leo Cooper, 1999)

Taylor, Phil and Pam Cupper, *Gallipoli: A Battlefield Guide*, (Kenthurst: Press Pty Ltd., 1989).

Thompson, Lieutenant-Colonel R. R., *The Fifty-Second (Lowland) Division, 1914-1918*, (Glasgow: Maclehose Jackson & Co, 1923).

Walker, R. W, *To What End Did They Die?: Officers Died at Gallipoli*, (Worcester: R. W. Walker Publishing., 1985).

INDEX

192